Goodbye, Friend

Goodbye, Friend

Healing Wisdom for Anyone
Who Has Ever Lost a Pet

GARY KOWALSKI

❋ STILLPOINT PUBLISHING
Walpole, New Hampshire

✳ STILLPOINT PUBLISHING
Your resource for books, audio tapes, and other
materials to "Live with an Awakened Spirit"

For a free catalog or ordering information, write:
Stillpoint Publishing, PO Box 640, Walpole, NH 03608, USA
or TOLL-FREE 800-847-4014 (USA) or 603-756-9281

This book is manufactured in the United States of America.
Cover design by Kathryn Sky-Peck
Text design by Heather Gendron

Library of Congress Cataloging-in-Publication Data:

Kowalski, Gary A.
        Goodbye, friend : healing wisdom for anyone who has ever lost a pet / Gary A. Kowalski - 1st ed.
        p.   cm.
        Includes bibliographical references (p. 157)
        ISBN: 1-883478-22-7
        1. Pet owners--Psychology. 2. Pets--Death--Psychological aspects. 3. Bereavement--Psychological aspects.   I. Title.
SF411.47.K68   1997
155.9'37--dc21   97-23101 CIP

1 3 5 7 9 8 6 4 2

This book is printed on acid-free recycled paper
to save trees and preserve Earth's ecology.

CONTENTS

———◆———

ACKNOWLEDGEMENTS

All the incidents recounted in this book are true. In some cases, minor details such as names have been changed to protect confidentiality or to simplify the narrative.

I want to thank the many individuals and organizations who contributed to this work, especially my wife Dori Jones, who helped with proofreading and offered her usual good advice, but also the following: Liz Frenette of the Monadnock Humane Society; David Walton, Ph.D.; Professor Jeanette Jones of Rutgers University (who besides conducting original research on the emotion of sadness happens to be my sister-in-law); Dawn Jones-Low (whose beautiful photographs do so much to enhance the text); Michael Ward; the International Association of Pet Cemeteries; Mount Auburn Cemetery in Cambridge, Massachusetts; Patricia Gabel of the Association for Gravestone Studies; Margaret Carter; Professor Robbie Kahn; Holly Cheever, D.V.M.; Holly Busier; Dee Kalea; Gloria Cooley; Errol Sowers, who contributed the story of his dog Lady; Ann Ashby, who shared her investigations on animal effigies and gravestone inscriptions; Connie Howard of the Greater Burlington Humane Society, who shared her own wisdom and permitted me to photograph animals in the shelter under her care; Iris Muggenthaler of Endtrap; Valerie Hurley and John Kern; and Professor Tom Regan of North Carolina State University. I especially thank Robbie Kahn of the University of Vermont for her insight that animals, like people, need emotional space and permission from their caregivers to depart on their own schedule. The information and help I received from these and others was invaluable.

I am also indebted to my congregation, the First Unitarian Universalist Society of Burlington, Vermont, for providing me with six months of sabbatical leave, which gave me time to undertake this project. I am grateful as well to the Harvard Divinity School for offering me a Merrill Fellowship in the spring of 1996, thus making it possible for me to use Harvard's libraries and other research facilities.

Finally, my appreciation goes to my publisher, Stillpoint Publishing, for the staff's editorial support and belief in the importance of this subject. My hope is that those who read this book will find consolation themselves and share this volume with others who are grieving. If the work brings a smile or helps to dry a tear, it will have been well worthwhile.

Some have left
and others are about to leave,
so why should we be sorry
that we too must go?
And yet our hearts are sad
that on this mighty road
the friends we meet can set
no place to meet again.

— FROM THE SANSKRIT,
TRANSLATED BY DANIEL INGALLS

1 PETS ARE NOT PETTY

Everything dies . . . goldfish, great blue whales, friends and people we love. There is a wistful sadness that accompanies the realization that all life must eventually come to an end. Accepting death and learning to live with joy in spite of it are difficult challenges. And this is true whether we are saying farewell to a person who has been close to us or to an animal that has been part of our family circle. The grief we feel when a relationship is severed can be intense.

This is a book for all those who have ever lost a cat, dog, or other animal companion. These creatures are commonly called pets, a word that is related to *petty*, meaning small, insignificant, or subordinate. For centuries, animals have been regarded as the inferiors of humankind. Some advocates of animal rights argue that we should eliminate the use of the word *pet* entirely for this reason. But of course *pet* can also mean favorite, cherished, especially near and dear, and it is for pet-lovers in this sense that this work is intended.

That includes most of us. When I was a theological student, in training for my eventual role as a clergyman, one of my professors warned the pupils in his preaching class never to mention the topic of dogs during a sermon. The reason? Listeners immediately begin to think of all the odd canine characters they have encountered over the years. Whatever point the minister was making is gone for good as the congregation is carried away in reverie and reminiscence.

There was Flush, for example, a springer spaniel named for Elizabeth Barrett Browning's more famous dog (who was the subject of a full-length biography by Virginia Wolff). My mother remembers Flush from her childhood during the Depression. In those lean times, meat was hard to come by, and the dog learned to love vegetables instead—the potato peels and carrot tops that were stewed for him, along with the fruit from the peach tree out back. His ears were so keen that he could hear the telltale plump of a peach when it plummeted in the night. He ate so many of the overripe desserts that his teeth were set on edge, and my mother vividly recalls the poor creature moaning because of his sore gums even as he gobbled down his goodies. Some brute finally poisoned him. But for my mom (who currently has no pets, nor does she even like dogs in general), the memories of Flush are still fresh, after more than sixty years.

Most of us have known a dog like that—or some other animal that has charmed its way into our hearts. The tears we shed when these creatures die are genuine, for our pets have an important place in our lives. Their gentle, trusting presence becomes a dependable part of our daily routine. They share our mealtimes and befriend us as playmates. They are with us on outings and adventures, and they accompany us in moments of quiet introspection. We sense the warmth of their affection and the depth of their loyalty, forming emotional bonds that can be as strong and nurturing as any in life. When these attachments are broken, we can experience a sense of emptiness and loss. We may feel depressed, numb, lost, or angry.

For some people, the death of a pet may represent the greatest loss they have ever encountered. Not long ago a college professor wrote to tell me about some informal research he conducted at the university where he taught for many years in West Virginia. It was his custom there to begin his introductory psychology classes by asking students to write down memories of a time when they felt most happy or sad. Among women, he found, the saddest events usually concerned the death of a grandparent or another close relative. For young men, rather curiously, the saddest memories typically involved the death of a dog. He says he was never able to fully probe that response to account for the gender difference. What was striking was that, when asked to recall their deepest personal sorrow, so many young adults would hearken back to the death of a pet.

Acknowledging loss and the feelings that go with it are an essential part of healing. Expressions of grief are the way we move through our pain, toward acceptance and resolution. We need the opportunity to cry, or shout, or shake our fists if we feel like it—all healthy forms of catharsis and emotional release. It hurts, and we need to say so.

Even more, we need to have our feelings affirmed by others. Of course, no one else can fix what's wrong. There are no magic words anyone can utter that will fill the gap left when a good friend dies. Pets would be petty indeed if their loss could be so easily overcome. But while no one else can take away our grief, the care and concern of others insures that we need not mourn alone. Knowing that others have wrestled with similar losses, our own sorrow becomes easier to bear.

Still, we may feel a little sheepish about sharing such a vulnerable part of ourselves. A reservation can arise—an inner doubt. Won't other people think it ridiculous to become so distraught over a mere animal? Some might consider it laughable. The humorist Garrison Keillor, for example, once wrote a comic sketch about the judge in a poetry contest who has to read through barrelfuls of bad verse, including some fairly amateurish elegies for departed critters. But even Mr. Keillor seems to understand that losing a pet can be wrenching and that there is nothing particularly funny about it. To his credit, he has written his own poem, "In Memory of Our Cat, Ralph."

> When we got home, it was almost dark.
> Our neighbor waited on the walk.
> "I'm sorry, I have bad news," he said.
> "Your cat, the gray-black one, is dead.
> I found him by the garage an hour ago."
> "Thank you," I said, "for letting us know."
>
> We dug a hole in the flower bed,
> The lilac bushes overhead,
> Where this cat loved to lie in spring
> And roll in the dirt and eat the green

Delicious first spring buds,
And laid him down and covered him up,
Wrapped in a piece of tablecloth,
Our good old cat laid in the earth.

We quickly turned and went inside
The empty house and sat and cried
Softly in the dark some tears
For that familiar voice, that fur,
That soft weight missing from our laps,
That we had loved too well perhaps
And mourned from weakness of the heart:
A childish weakness, to regard
An animal whose life is brief
With such affection and such grief.

"If this is foolish," Keillor writes in his final stanza, "so it be." But it is not foolish or childish—merely human. Our sense of loss deserves to be respected, not belittled.

Fortunately, more and more counselors, clergy, and therapists are beginning to realize this. Some humane societies now offer grief groups for those who have lost an animal companion. For those who need a listening ear, the veterinary school at the University of California in Davis offers a telephone hotline, a service the staff there would like to see replicated in other portions of the country. You can join pet loss groups on the Internet. Some companies that manufacture stationery even have a special sympathy cards for the occasion.

Yet still more is needed. At last count, there were sixty-four million household cats in the United States, and fifty-five million dogs, with an untold assortment of gerbils, rabbits, parrots, and other pets. Every year thousands of people suffer inwardly because they are without solace or support when their animals die. For those who want a healing connection, this book is one more point of contact.

Can a book help? In *Winnie the Pooh*, the author A.A. Milne describes a situation in which Pooh, after eating several jars of honey, becomes stuck in the entrance of his friend Rabbit's burrow. Although the residents of the Hundred Acre Wood push and pull, he is jammed so tightly that he cannot budge. With a sigh and a tear, the overweight bear realizes that he will have to remain in the hole, on a strict diet, until he is slim enough to come out. He resigns himself, with one final request. "Would you read a Sustaining Book," he earnestly asks Christopher Robin, "such as would comfort a Wedged Bear in Great Tightness?"

To all those who feel stuck, in apathy or resentment or just down in the dumps, these pages are dedicated. Perhaps they will help you out of whatever hole you are in. And what holds true for bears may also pertain to books: fatter is not always better. For while this is a slim volume, its aim and subject—grieving and recovering after the loss of a pet—are anything but petty.

I have done mostly what most men do,
And pushed it out of my mind;
But I can't forget, if I wanted to,
Four-Feet trotting behind.

Day after day, the whole day through—
Wherever my road inclined—
Four-Feet said, "I am coming with you!"
And trotted along behind.

— "FOUR-FEET" BY RUDYARD KIPLING

2 Four-Footed Comforters

As a parish minister, I know how hard it is to lose a beloved dog or cat. People often turn to me for comfort when their pets die. I once received a hand-written note just a few moments before our morning worship service was to begin: would I please announce that "Oatmeal," the canine companion of a woman attending our church, had passed away the previous week? Oatmeal had been an old dog, much loved by his mistress, who apparently felt the loss keenly.

Briefly, I debated with myself. I wondered how others in the congregation would react to including such an item among the joys and concerns we normally share on Sunday morning. Would they consider such an announcement out of place? I was glad that I followed my instincts, for several weeks later I received another note thanking me for acknowledging Oatmeal's death. Simply having her sorrow recognized and validated in a religious setting proved deeply comforting to the dog's owner.

I use this term "owner" with hesitation. We may be the legal custodians of our animal companions, and responsible for their well-being, but while animals may be many things—cantankerous, humorous, neurotic, or supremely

sane—they are never merely property. They are hardly in
the same category as personal possessions. Many people
think of pets as members of their extended family. As any
animal lover can testify, they have likes and dislikes, moods
and feelings that are very much like our own.

In this connection, it is interesting to realize that we are
not the only animals who grieve. Other species appear to
have at least an incipient understanding of death and may
experience all the pangs of separation when a loved one
dies. For example, in his book *Lucy: Growing Up Human,*
Maurice Temerlin tells how the chimpanzee he and his wife
had reared from infancy reacted to the discovery that her
pet cat had met its end:

> I was in the courtyard at the time and I
> heard a scream coming from inside Lucy's
> roof-top room. It was a different kind of
> scream from any I had ever heard and I
> rushed immediately to the roof of the house.
> The cat was dead on the floor, of undeter-
> mined causes. Lucy was at the other end of
> the room, obviously quite shaken.

The two animals had been inseparable friends, and Lucy
was clearly affected. She stared at the body fixedly, tentatively
raised a finger as if to touch it, but then withdrew her hand
with a nervous shake without making contact. Three
months later, leafing through a copy of *Psychology Today*
(her foster father, Maurice, was a therapist), the ape came
across an article on chimps that happened to include a
photo of herself and the deceased kitten. For five minutes,

Lucy sat immobile, then began to gesture rapidly over and over in American Sign Language: "Lucy's cat, Lucy's cat. . . ." Sadness is apparently not a uniquely human response to death. Even a chimp can miss its companion and may go on mourning for quite some time.

Some animals appear to shed tears as we do. In his book *Crying: The Mystery of Tears*, Dr. William Frey reports one case of this phenomenon. A woman in Texas had a dog that was killed by a car. Afterward, the woman's other dog lay on the site of the grave for weeks, with large tears rolling down its face. Such anecdotes are common, Frey notes, and although some experts dispute their veracity, there is little reason to doubt that whether they actually shed tears or not, other creatures react to loss with anxiety and alarm, much as we do. In a very literal sense, therefore, it is natural for us to weep at the time of death. It may be an instinctive response to bereavement, one common to many species. For me it is comforting to know that, in our struggle to come to terms with loss, we human beings are not alone.

But in our culture it is not easy to grieve or say good-bye. Especially in the case of animals, the suffering we experience may be minimized. While a death in the human community is almost always attended with some rituals of mourning, the passing of a dog or cat is seldom marked by any solemn rites. Condolences can be expected when a person dies, but in the case of a pet we are less apt to receive any expressions of sympathy or understanding. While friends and family gather for support in the event of a human death, those who grieve for a pet will likely go home at night to a house that feels empty and abandoned. A few people may empathize, but many will not. We will probably be expected to carry on with our work and other day-to-day responsibilities as though nothing serious has happened.

Yet the loss of a friend is always cause for concern. We know, for instance, that animals can play a significant role in human health. Studies show that the simple act of stroking a dog or cat, or even just holding an animal in one's lap, can slow the pulse rate and lower blood pressure. (The combination of touch and talk with an animal seems even more beneficial than similar contact with another human being.) People who have pets have a lower risk of heart disease and tend to live longer than people who lack such companionship. One experiment showed that even sitting quietly in front of an aquarium can have positive physiological effects, much like meditation.

Pets are good medicine. I came to a firsthand appreciation of this many years ago, when I worked in a halfway house for people with mental illness. One of our residents was a young woman named Peggy, who was about nineteen years old. She had long brown hair and a beautiful, shy smile. She had tried to cut her wrists more times than I care to remember. Diagnosed with schizophrenia, Peggy lived in a world of her own that neither I nor the other counselors or psychiatrists who worked with her could fully enter. Her lifeline was her dog, a pure white Samoyed named Alfonse.

So long as Alfonse was thriving and well cared for, we knew that Peggy was all right. Grooming, feeding, and walking the dog were the points of stability and wellness in

Peggy's life. Whenever the dog was neglected, however, it was a sign Peggy had become self-destructive and might be in danger of hurting herself. Alfonse was in a certain sense Peggy's *alter ego*—a four-legged, furry window into her otherwise hidden inner life.

Small wonder that animals have now become a standard feature in many hospitals and other therapeutic environments. Where else can we find such unconditional regard or such sweet spontaneity? Animals seem to know when we are hurting and instinctively care for us in times of need. Michael Ward, who lives in North Carolina, wrote me a letter not long ago that convinced me of this. "My girlfriend was going through a very hard time in her life," he explains.

> I tried to console her as best I could, but sometimes words are not enough. She asked to stay over that night so she wouldn't be alone at her apartment. She lay down, ready to go to sleep, and what happened next amazed me. My dog, Grish, jumped in bed, laid his massive black lab head down on her stomach, and stayed there all night. He has never done that before or since.

Many have had similar experiences. In one remarkable case, a boy who was comatose and who had resisted all previous efforts at resuscitation finally regained consciousness thanks to his pet dog Rusty. The child, a victim of head injury, had been unconscious for ten days. As family members in the hospital room discussed various matters that included mention of the dog, they noticed a slight change of expression on the boy's face. After conferring with doctors, they brought the animal to the hospital room. The boy then reawakened as Rusty began to lick his hands and face. In less dramatic ways, as well, our pets help us through hard times. "In dark hours," the poet W.H. Auden wrote of his dog Rolfi, "your silence may be of more help than many two-legged comforters."

It can be shattering when these creatures die. We may feel as though we had lost a part of ourselves. Unfortunately, there is no instant repair kit for the soul, nor any simple method that can be mechanically followed to restore oneself to wholeness. Each person's grieving is likely to be singular. There is something unpredictable (and yet dependable) about the process.

Grief and healing are both a part of the current of life, moving at their own ordained pace. No one, for instance, can say how long we will mourn. Grieving may commonly be measured in days or weeks, but it can be months, or even longer. Many people report feeling "choked up" by the memory of a beloved pet years after the animal is gone. Some mental health professionals suppose that feelings of sadness will usually dissipate within a week or two (much of the literature labels extended grieving as "pathological"), but in many cases they underestimate the pain involved.

After more than two decades, my friend Iris still has a catch in her voice when she talks about her horse, "Sentimental Journey" (the title of a song that was popular when she named him as a foal.) She shared the prime of life with him, from the time she was sixteen until her middle forties. The dailiness of that twenty-nine-year relationship and the physical immediacy of it created a visceral bond, she says, that was even stronger than the one she shared with family. "He was more of a permanent fixture in my life than parents, school, even husband and child," she notes. "How could his death not affect me?"

Iris has since then owned other horses, as well as several dogs (when one shows signs of aging, she now adopts another animal to ease the transition), a calf that was rescued from the slaughterhouse—it finally died of heart problems, but at least had a shot at life—and even a raccoon named Harry, which broke its neck in a fall. It is hard to conceive of enduring that much loss. But Iris, who has been the leader of our statewide effort to ban the leghold trap—a cause she adopted when one of her own pets was mangled by one of these mischievous devices—cares passionately about animals. For her, life without this varied menagerie would be even harder to imagine.

"Until one has loved an animal," wrote Anatole France, "a part of one's soul remains unawakened." Almost anyone who has ever let an animal under his or her skin will agree that for all the aggravations and heartaches that come with having a pet, the return in love, affection, and memory can make it all worthwhile.

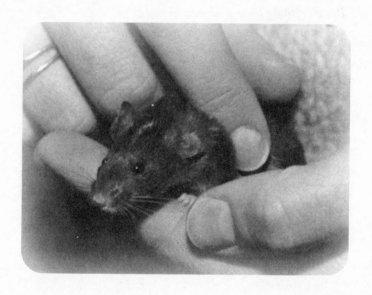

―――――•―――――

For everything there is a season,
and a time for every matter under the sun:
A time to be born and a time to die;
A time to plant, and a time to pluck up what is planted;
A time to kill and a time to heal;
A time to break down and a time to build up;
A time to weep and a time to laugh;
A time to mourn and a time to dance.
A generation comes, and a generation goes,
but the earth remains forever.
For everything there is a season,
and a time to every purpose under heaven.

— ECCLESIASTES

―――――•―――――

3 To Everything There Is a Season

With more than five hundred members in my congregation, I can count on a fair number of babies being born each year, as well a certain number of people dying. Part of my job is to conduct the memorial whenever a death occurs. Although each service is different and tailored to the circumstances, I begin many of them with the same reading. I have recited the words of Ecclesiastes so often that I can recall most of them from memory: "To everything there is a season, and a time for every purpose under heaven."

It helps me to remember that our lives proceed according to a natural rhythm. The same forces that turn the seasons and move the planets carry us in their unfolding. Stars have their lifespan, and we have ours. Even the earth, which seemed to the ancient writers of the Bible to outlast time, was young once and will ultimately grow old. It's how the world stays in balance and makes room for the new.

Each living thing has its own distinct season and duration. Among mammals, a well-known rule holds that small creatures have the briefest tenure on the earth; larger ones live longer. So a mouse or gerbil might live a year or two, a dolphin twenty to fifty, depending on the species, a human being threescore and ten. As body weight increases, life expectancy also tends to go up (.28 times as fast, to be exact). If the universe were kinder, the lifespan of a dog or cat might be closer to our own. As it is, loss is built into the equation. From the moment we become attached to the pets who play such an important part in our lives, we know the day will come when we have to say farewell.

Built-in limits appear to govern how long any organism can live. Among *Homo sapiens*, the maximum age that has ever been reliably documented is 114 years, and although in the last century the average life expectancy of men and women in economically developed nations has increased, no one expects the record to be pushed much higher. Human cells, when cultured in the laboratory, can divide and reproduce only a finite number of times. This means that the tissues in the body eventually lose their ability to repair and regenerate themselves. As in a car with an odometer that has turned over once too often, things just wear out.

Some pets can be exceptionally long-lived. One dog named Bluey, owned by Les Hall of Victoria, Australia, reputedly lived to the ripe old age of 29 years and 5 months, while the record-holding cat, a female tabby in Great Britain, was said to be 34 years old when she finally died in 1957. But few dogs or cats will live to such an advanced age, nor should they. The better part of wisdom lies in accepting nature's limits.

Time restrictions apply to all of us, two-legged and four-legged. In his book *How We Die,* physician Sherwin Nuland observes that while human death certificates must legally stipulate a specific cause of death (stroke, cancer, pneumonia, etc.), many people simply die of old age. Eventually, one ailment or another is bound to overmaster the fading defenses of a tired body.

Although the catalogue of maladies would differ for other species, the principle is the same. Heart attacks among dogs and cats are rare, for instance. Having evolved as carnivores, they can handle the cholesterol that blocks and hardens human arteries and results in cardiac arrest. Degenerative heart diseases are common, however. The heart is a pump and like any mechanical device tends to break down over time. Valves start to leak, and as pumping capacity is reduced, other organs (like the kidneys and liver) are insufficiently supplied with blood and also begin to fail, creating additional complications.

Experts estimate that from twenty to thirty percent of dogs over the age of nine exhibit some degree of congestive heart disease. But those animals that are lucky enough to escape it will eventually fall victim to other illnesses. Cancer and arthritis are common causes of death among canines. The afflictions of older cats include cancer, hyperthyroidism, kidney disease, and diabetes. But the truth is that many animals perish because they have plain run out of steam.

According to the law of entropy—one of the fundamental assertions of modern physics—everything decays. High-energy systems tend to move toward low-energy. A watch that is left to itself, for instance, runs down. Without outside intervention—someone to wind it, or put in a new battery—it stays unwound. In some cases, outside interventions can also prolong a life; medical science proves it. But like a watch, even if the mainspring holds and the gears don't rust, we are all running out of time.

Some think the ticking of the clock may be genetically determined. That would explain why people whose parents are long-lived tend to be chronologically gifted themselves. It would also provide a reason for species with differing genetic make-up to display such markedly different life expectancies. As demonstrated in the accompanying table on "Comparative Lifespans for Companion Animals," the average length of life for both common and exotic pets varies widely, depending mostly on their size.

Comparative Lifespans for Companion Animals

Mice	1.5–3 years
Hamsters	1.5–2 years
Gerbils	3–4 years
Rats	2.5–3.5 years
Guinea Pigs	4–5 years
Rabbits	5–6 years
Ferrets	5–8 years
Hedgehogs	6–10 years
Cats	13–17 years
Dogs	11–13 years
Pot-Bellied Pigs	20–25 years
Horses	20–30 years

Large mammals live longer, although exceptions occur. Dogs are bigger than cats, but typically don't live quite as long. And human beings live even longer than their relatively large size would indicate. Our unusual longevity is both a blessing and burden, since it means we have more time to enjoy life but must also mourn those who pass more quickly through the world.

Of course, the quality of a life can never be measured by mere quantity. People now live longer than their grandparents, but are they any more content? While I might or might not last as long as a humpback whale, which can easily live to be a hundred, I will probably never be as serene—as benign and tolerant—as one of those mellow giants. And although twelve years—the actuarial average for river otters—seems rather short, I might willingly shave a few years off my lifespan in return for half their *joie de vivre*. What counts, after all, is not living long so much as living well.

While the life expectancy of various species may differ, all might be said to enjoy the same amount of "biological time" between birth and death. Harvard biologist Stephen Jay Gould points out that because metabolic rates differ on the same scale as size and longevity, a mouse will experience as many heartbeats during its brief lifetime as an elephant will in its more prolonged existence. A dog, a cat, a horse, and a hamster will all inhale and exhale—draw breath into the lungs and release it again—about the same number of times during their markedly different lifespans. Everyone gets roughly the same share: 800 million heartbeats, or 200 million lungfuls.

Each species appears to experience time according to its own inner rhythm, just as animals age and grow at different rates. A dog, for example, matures on its own timetable. While people may speak casually of one "dog year" equaling seven human years, no one-to-one comparisons can be made. In his imperfect motor skills and boundless curiosity, a six-month-old puppy is like a child of six, while a one-year-old dog might be considered the equivalent of a teenager, having sexually matured within the space of twelve months.

The dog's pace of growth slows after two years, however. From that point on, one canine year amounts to about four of our own. By the time a dog reaches twelve, its physical condition is similar to that of a person rapidly approaching seventy—one nearing the end of his or her normal lifespan. But while the life of another animal might seem short to us, it is surely complete and fulfilling within its own frame of reckoning. It moves along at its own proper gait.

Life is fleeting, and any loss, whether it be the death of a person or a pet, tends to make us aware of the brevity of existence. Death prompts us to self-examination. Are we getting the most out of life? What more do we need to do or be or accomplish for our own lifetimes to feel complete? Are there places to go, people to see, or things to learn before we leave the world? If so, there is no time like the present. Becoming more conscious of death can make us more conscious of life as well, inviting us to reflect on the way we will spend the limited years we have available.

Nothing lives forever, but within its allotted span, every creature—the mayfly that perishes in a day as well as the redwood that survives a thousand years—has equal opportunity to savor its moment in the sun. It is a thought that helps me make peace with death, which almost always comes too soon, for us and for the animals we love. "To everything there is a season, and a time for every purpose under heaven."

A faithful friend is a strong protection.
A person who has found one has found a treasure.
A faithful friend is beyond price,
And his value cannot be weighed.
A faithful friend is a life-giving medicine.

—THE APOCRYPHA

4 Kindness Begins At Home

Dogs have been called man's best friend—but other creatures also make equally fine companions. When they are gone, we may have to work a little harder than usual to be compassionate with ourselves. We have to be our own best friends.

One of the reasons we value pets is that they help keep us grounded. Our companion animals exemplify healthy living. When I begin to worry excessively, my dog can pull me out of my brooding and help put my problems in proper perspective. If I become overly serious, he invites me to join in frolicking and play. Because animals have wants that are few and basic, they can help teach us to slow down, simplify, and concentrate on the essentials. Particularly at a time of loss, we need to pay extra attention to taking care of our own animal needs. For instance:

Animals need to eat. So do you, even if in your grieving you seem to have little appetite.

Animals need to exercise. Remember that you do, too. Take a walk or go to the gym, even though you may feel listless or worn down.

Animals need to sleep. A physical workout will help you get a good night's rest, which is often a problem for people who are upset.

Animals need to have fun. If you especially enjoy certain activities, make sure to build them into your schedule.

Animals need companionship. Try to make an extra effort to to reach out to others at a time of separation, when you are likely to feel especially isolated.

Another lesson animals teach us is the importance of routine. My dog Chinook, for instance, likes his meals at the proper intervals, with punctual trips to the park in the morning and evening hours. Unless it's an extra biscuit at bedtime, the ideal day for him holds few or no surprises.

Routines are important to people, too. For this reason, it is not usually a good idea to make any major decisions in the period immediately following a loss. Our judgment frequently suffers when we are under stress. If possible, postpone making any big changes in your life. Stick to the familiar. This is probably not the moment to replace your pet, for instance, nor is it the time to vow that you will never have another. Allow yourself time to absorb and adjust to the situation.

At the same time, when we suffer a loss our routines will invariably be disrupted. A death means that the pattern of life has changed. Ingrained habits—going for a walk with the dog every evening, setting out food for the cat before work—will serve as persistent reminders of the loss that has befallen us. Like a person who has been recently widowed and automatically makes two cups of coffee instead of one, we may have to be retrained. Paradoxically, we may spend more time thinking about our pets after they are gone than we did while they were alive. They become noticeable by their absence.

One loss accentuates others. I think in this regard of Amy, who shared a cup of coffee with me not long ago. Amy lost her cat last fall. Mittens was quite old, although neither Amy nor her friend Chris was sure of his precise age, since fifteen years ago he simply showed up and moved in, quite as if he owned the place. Amy and Chris were living together in an old farmhouse, and the twosome became a threesome. They went on picnics together and shared vacations. Amy and Chris even talked about getting married, but the plans were always postponed, and eventually Chris took a promotion that required him to move to another city. At thirty-seven, Amy's dream of having a family now seems to be fading. Months have passed, but she still misses Mittens. The cat's death put a period on an important chapter of her life.

Each of us carries longstanding loads of disappointment and disillusion, and any loss can open old wounds. Depending on their situation, some people will be harder hit by death than others. Those who live alone or who have no dependents, for example, may be especially affected. One of our basic human satisfactions is the feeling of being needed, and attending to an animal gives many people a daily sense of being useful. It is important to know you make a difference, at least to one appreciative creature. For such people, losing a pet can mean losing a sense of purpose.

For the elderly, the death of a pet can be a reminder of their own mortality. For adolescents, who may feel misunderstood by parents and estranged from other family members, a dog or cat may be the only trusted friend in whom they can confide. For couples that are childless or whose children have left the nest, an animal will often become a surrogate son or daughter. In each case, coping with pet loss can be difficult.

Some pets may be more deeply missed than others. In one study at the University of Pennsylvania, trained bereavement counselors were paired with people who were mourning for their pets, in an effort to understand more about this kind of loss. The research showed that individuals who lose a cat may have a more severe grief reaction and need greater follow-up than those who lose a dog. It seems peculiar. Do cats, as creatures that can be perfectly happy living in a small apartment, tend to be adopted more frequently by people who live alone and lack social networks? Or does one's relationship with a cat tend to be more nuanced and understated, leaving a greater residue of "unfinished business" when the animal dies? Since the reasons for the finding are unclear, we should not give the study more weight than it deserves. What is certain is that both cats and dogs, as well as other pets, have a lasting claim on our affection.

It is equally certain that any change in our personal lives or any rupture in our relationships creates stress. The resulting turmoil takes a toll on our biological and psychological defenses. The pioneering work in this area was done in 1967 by the psychologists Thomas Holmes and R.H. Rahe, who developed a "Social Readjustment Scale" (first published in the *Journal of Psychosomatic Research*, and reproduced here) that assigns various points to the major traumas and minor calamities that make up the wear and tear of existence. You may want to use this instrument to determine your own stress level. The higher your score, the greater the threat to your personal health and well-being.

The death of a spouse is considered to be the most grievous loss, receiving the most points. Divorce, unemployment, hospitalization, relocation, financial losses, and other upheavals receive relatively fewer points on the scale, down to minor infractions of the law. For whatever reason, those who devised the scale did not feel the death of a companion animal was important enough to be included among the other strains of normal living. Perhaps the researchers considered such a loss inconsequential—less stressful even than receiving a speeding ticket. Unfortunately, many people act as though animals do not (or should not) matter.

Goodbye, Friend

The Social Readjustment Rating Scale

Life Event	*Mean Stress Value*

1. Death of Spouse 100
2. Divorce 73
3. Marital separation from mate 65
4. Detention in jail or other institution 63
5. Death of a close family member 63
6. Major personal injury or illness......................................53
7. Marriage 50
8. Being fired at work..47
9. Marital reconciliation with mate...............................45
10. Retirement from work 45
11. Major change in health or behavior
    of a family member 44
12. Pregnancy 40
13. Sexual difficulties...39
14. Gaining a new family member (through
    birth, adoption, oldster moving in, etc.)...............................39
15. Major business readjustment (merger, reorganization,
    bankruptcy, etc.) 39
16. Major change in financial state (a lot worse off or
    a lot better off than usual)..38
17. Death of a close friend 37
18. Changing to a different line of work............................36
19. Major change in the number of
    arguments with spouse 35
20. Taking out a mortgage for a loan or a major purchase........31
21. Foreclosure on a mortgage or loan................................30
22. Major change in responsibilities at work (promotion,
    demotion, lateral transfer) 29

But of course they do matter. When clinicians interviewed middle-aged couples who had lost a household pet, most agreed it was a painful event, less stressful than the death of an immediate family member but more stressful than the death of other relatives. One study in Great Britain discovered that ten percent of those who lost a pet developed symptoms severe enough to warrant a visit to the doctor. This finding is consistent with the work of Holmes and Rahe, who discovered that individuals who accumulated more than 300 points on the social readjustment scale within a twelve-month period had an eighty percent likelihood of falling ill, either physically or mentally, while about half of those who scored between 150 and 299 could also expect to get sick.

Like anyone else who has suffered a blow, people whose animals have died are at increased risk. One follow-up study of individuals mourning the loss of a companion animal found that in the weeks immediately following the death, more than ninety percent of owners experienced some disruption of their sleep habits or had difficulty eating—both symptoms of clinical depression. More than half became withdrawn and avoided social activities. Almost fifty percent encountered job-related difficulties, missing from one to three days of work as a result of listlessness or low energy. There is even some indication that married couples are more likely to separate or divorce after the death of a household pet. All these symptoms suggest that the loss of a pet is serious business, with potential to adversely affect one's health, career, and other relationships.

My standard advice to anyone who is grieving is, "Take care of yourself." Eat right. Get plenty of rest. If possible, take some time off from work, or if you can't do that, find other opportunities for relaxation and recuperation. Be good to your body. You may be depressed when your best friend dies; you can be exhausted and on edge. You have every right to feel that way. But try to treat yourself at least as well as you would any other injured and hurting creature. Remember, the precept "Be Kind To Animals" applies not just to the four-legged variety. It applies to you as well.

Hear our humble prayer, O God, for our friends, the animals. Especially for animals who are suffering; for any that are hunted or lost or deserted or frightened or hungry; for all that must be put to death. We entreat for them all thy mercy and pity. And for those who deal with them, we ask a heart of compassion, gentle and kindly words. Make us true friends of the animals and so to share the blessings of the merciful.

— ALBERT SCHWEITZER

5 WHEN BAD THINGS HAPPEN TO GOOD CREATURES

I consider my dog to be pretty smart, but he can be awfully dumb about cars. When he was younger, I spent hours training him to respond to commands—sit, heel, stay, and come—and he is generally good about doing as I ask. But more than once, he has ambled recklessly into the street, oblivious equally to my shouts and whistles and to the oncoming traffic.

Luckily, he has always escaped serious injury. But that did not keep me from becoming agitated on such occasions. Once I saw that he was out of danger and my initial panic had passed, I was annoyed with my dog for failing to obey and irritated with myself for allowing such a dangerous situation to arise in the first place. I can only imagine how upset I would be if he were ever hurt.

Unfortunately, thousands of animals are killed every year in accidents, usually involving an automobile. When a pet dies needlessly and painfully, or simply disappears without returning, it is especially hard to accept the loss. Anger, guilt, and "if-onlys" can cloud the horizon.

The depth of feeling present on such occasions came to light some years ago when Richard Joseph wrote a letter to the editor of his local newspaper after a speeding car hit his dog Vicky. Addressed "To the Man Who Killed My Dog," the letter touched such a sensitive nerve that it was reprinted in papers all over the country.

"I hope you were going some place important when you drove so fast down Cross Highway across Bayberry Lane, Tuesday night," the letter began:

> Maybe we'd feel better if we could imagine that you were a doctor rushing somewhere to deliver a baby or ease somebody's pain. . . . But even though all we saw of you was the black shadow of your car and its jumping red tail lights as you roared down the road, we know too much about you to believe it. You saw the dog, you stepped on your brakes, you felt a thump, you heard a yelp, then my wife's scream. Your reflexes are better than your heart and stronger than your courage— we know that—because you jumped on the gas again and got out of there as fast as your car could carry you.

True, the dog's owner had lost his grip on the leash for a moment as he was closing the garden gate, and in just that instant the puppy darted into the road where it met its end. Joseph reproached himself for his own carelessness in the matter. But it was the driver's responsibility to stop when the accident occurred. It was hard for Joseph not to feel bitter.

Within weeks, Richard Joseph had received hundreds of sympathy letters from people who had also lost pets and were struggling with similar emotions of frustration and incompletion: The blow is sudden and unexpected, the culprit often unknown. There may be no time for leave-taking. Those who suffered similar losses knew how ragged and shaken he was feeling after the accident.

Joseph's experience taught him several things about grief and healing. Seeing his dog killed by a hit-and-run driver almost destroyed his faith in human nature. How could anyone could be so callous? On the other hand, the outpouring of encouragement and support he received from countless strangers told him that a solid bedrock of decency remains in most people.

It also reminded Joseph of the necessity for transforming misfortune into opportunity. "Loss creates sorrow," he observed, "sorrow frequently turns bitter and becomes anger, and anger destroys not only its object but the person who harbors it." Through his letter, he was able not only to vent and release his anger but perhaps also to help millions of people become a bit more careful behind the wheel. If it caused one driver to avoid one accident, he said, he would be satisfied with the outcome.

Writing a letter can be a good way to get things off your chest. Richard Joseph, as it happened, was a literary craftsman, a travel writer by trade, and could precisely gauge the impact of his message. Most of us are not as adept at weighing our words, and it is not usually a good idea to actually mail a letter written in the heat of passion. But just articulating our indignation can help. Write your letter, and then throw it away, or tell a friend just how angry you are. Express your animosity—pound the mattress if need be. Honor your anger, but let it go.

Anger and aggression usually erupt when we sense that we are out of control. All of us want to shape and manage our own destiny, and death represents an absolute affront to that desire. We may feel angry at our pet ("Why did he have to run into the street instead of coming when I called?"), put out by events that appear arbitrary or irrational ("I'd like to wring that driver's neck. Why was she talking on the car phone instead of watching the road?"), or mad at God, who seems to be responsible for making a world where accidents and other bad things happen. One woman told me that after one of her dogs died, she felt a temporary surge of hostility toward her two other animals who were left behind, as if unconsciously asking the question, "Why are you still alive while my favorite is now gone?" Only after a friend pointed out that she was not treating her remaining pets very well did she realize how resentful she was feeling and how her reaction was distancing her from companions who might have been supporting her at a time of loss.

But wherever our anger is directed, the physiology is much the same. When threatened, our reflexes kick in, and the autonomic nervous system, which governs involuntary organs, takes over. The heart rate rises, breathing becomes rapid, and muscles contract in preparation for fight or flight. Unfortunately, staying angry does nothing to put us back in command of the situation. Instead, we are merely reacting to events and letting them control us.

Anger is one of the predictable stages of grief. First comes a sense of shock or numbness, often followed by disbelief and denial ("This can't really be happening!"). Once the mourner has accepted the reality of the situation, the pain of separation begins. Many feelings can surface at this point, for grief is not itself an emotion but the whole constellation of responses that arise in time of loss. Rage, anxiety, helplessness, and other sensations are common.

Such suffering cannot be avoided. Often, the emotions come in waves; at unexpected moments, the bereaved person may be overcome with tears. But if ebb and flow of emotion is given scope and not suppressed, the waves of despondency become less frequent and less acute. With enough time, the mourner picks up the pieces and begins to rebuild the structures of everyday life. Eventually he or she can use the energy from the bonds that were broken to reinvest in new relationships.

Speaking of stages is naturally descriptive rather than prescriptive. Everyone's experience is different, and all feelings are valid. But it may help to know that if you are feeling furious, that is not unusual. And if you are tired of being angry and in conflict with the world, it is equally useful to know that such discordant, tumultuous feelings need not last forever.

When bad things happen, it is normal to feel bereft, bewildered, or betrayed. You are entitled to be upset. But life also requires that we forgive and move on. As Richard Joseph discovered, if you can find a constructive outlet for your anger, you will not only feel better in the long run; you may also help to make the world a slightly better place.

—◆—

See, Lord,
my coat hangs in tatters,
like homespun, old, threadbare.
All that I had of zest,
all my strength,
I have given in hard work
and kept nothing back for myself.
Now
my poor head swings
to offer up all the loneliness of my heart.
Dear God,
stiff on my thickened legs
I stand here before You:
Your unprofitable servant.
Oh! of Your goodness,
give me a gentle death.
Amen

— "Prayer of the Old Horse"
by Carmen Bernos De Gasztold

—◆—

6 A GOOD DEATH

While death is sometimes accidental, it is often deliberately chosen, as an act of kindness, for people as for animals. But even when death is welcomed, it is seldom easy for those who remain behind.

A friend of mine, for instance, recently lost her father, whose health had been declining for many years. He not only had Alzheimer's and diabetes, he also suffered an assortment of other ailments that finally meant he could live only with the benefit of artificial life support. He had no real hope of recovery. At last the point came when his family decided to end the struggle and withdraw the machines.

Death in this case might have been experienced as a release. The time had come to go. But it was still extremely painful for my friend to sit by her father's bedside and watch the monitors recording his blood pressure slowly fall to zero as his life slipped away. The person she was closest to was gone forever. An important part of her own history had receded into the past.

Even when death is consciously chosen, it may still come with a sense of resignation and regret. When we decide to euthanize an animal, the same mixture of feelings can be present, along with a similar array of questions:

Am I doing the right thing? Are there any realistic alternatives? What would I want if I were a sick and hurting animal and could think through the choices before me? When our pets are in chronic discomfort, or become immobilized and can no long enjoy the activities that once gave them pleasure, we realize that the quality of their lives is diminished.

But it may still be difficult or impossible to empathize fully or to understand how an illness is experienced from the pet's point of view. While animals clearly feel pain, do they suffer the same kind of psychological distress that humans normally associate with declining health? When do we continue treatment, and at what point does the struggle become too costly, financially or emotionally? Because these are the kinds of questions that have no precise answers, we can rely only on our own judgment, along with the advice of a veterinarian. We have ample room for self-doubt and second thoughts.

Once the decision has been made to euthanize, we can take certain steps to minimize the anguish involved, both for ourselves and for our animals. Being present at the time of death is clearly important, for even if it is hard to watch our animals put down, it must be still more difficult to live with the unanswered questions that arise from not knowing: Did the end come quickly? Were the last moments tense or peaceful?

For a few people, the thought of witnessing their animals die may be too troubling to contemplate. And in some cases, a veterinarian may ask for privacy; it can be tricky to find the vein in a small animal whose pulse hardly registers, particularly with an over-anxious pet owner hovering nearby. But in general, people can offer caring and reassurance to their pets until the final moment of life, thanks to veterinarians who have become increasingly sensitive to the emotional needs of pet owners. Some vets will even make house calls to administer the final injection to an ailing animal. More and more people are now choosing to die at home, in familiar surroundings rather than in the antiseptic atmosphere of a hospital. Why shouldn't we give our animals the same option?

Like my friend, who wanted to be near her father's bedside at the end of life, even if the vigil was lonely and disquieting, we often need to be close to our companions, for their sake as well as our own. We can also assist our pets toward the transition of death. No one knows how much a cat or dog really understands of what we say (more than we suspect, is my guess), but by speaking to them gently and explaining very simply what lies ahead—one shot, followed by drowsiness, then relief from pain and rest for weary bodies—they can certainly intuit the emotional substance behind our words.

By way of analogy: I almost always talk to my dog if I know I am going out of town. I typically tell him where I am headed, how long I will be gone, what arrangements I have made for his care, and when I will be back. Whether he comprehends all the details is unimportant if I have done my best to communicate that things will be okay. He seems calmed by the conversation.

And while death represents a permanent separation rather than a temporary one, the principle still holds. We can let our animals know that they are going on a trip, to a place with no struggle and no suffering. We can tell them how much we will miss them and what a special place they will always have in our lives. We can hug them and hold them. Through what we say and how we say it we can express our love for them rather than our need for them, giving them permission to depart on their own timetable rather than insisting that they remain here for our sake. From our tone of voice, they may sense that a major change is in the offing, but they may also understand that we will remain with them to the end and that there is ultimately nothing to fear.

Animals often understand more of these matters than most people imagine. I came to that conclusion after talking with Dawn, a veterinary technician with a degree in zoology who has long experience working with animals. When her horse Hastings had to be euthanized, she was very intentional about the event. She invited several friends to be with her and create a circle of caring and support. (Asking others to accompany you through this difficult passage is almost always a good idea.) Once all were present, she helped the weakened animal through a final dressage, the set of equestrian manuevers that in the days of his strength were Hastings' pride and joy. She assured the horse, with words and actions, how much she cared for him. Afterward, the company walked to a lower pasture where the earth had already been made hollow. It was a harmonious exit, well-planned and gently administered, as unperturbed as a tide flowing out to sea. When Dawn returned to the barn after the veterinarian had done his work, the other horses there all begun to whicker softly, in the same breathy tones they might use to comfort a troubled colt. Apparently, they knew that their herdmate was gone and wanted to offer comfort to Dawn, as well as to each other, in whatever way they could.

Perhaps our animals can guide us as well as console us at such times. For if most organisms have an innate survival instinct that drives them to cling to life against all odds, many also seem to possess an inborn sense that tells them when the time has come to let go and bow to the inevitable. That, at least, was the experience of one of my acquaintances, who told me about her mare Kalea.

Although the horse had enjoyed fifteen years of good health and would normally be considered only middle-aged, Kalea had developed a severe illness, apparently a case of plant poisoning, which gradually damaged her liver. She had become so emaciated and weak that she actually hesitated to lie down, knowing that she might not have the strength to stand again. For some time, she had willingly allowed the vet to daily insert a nasogastric tube delivering food and medicine. This day, uncharacteristically, Kalea refused the vet's care. Although her human caregivers could have forced the issue, they decided instead to respect Kalea's wishes. "We both knew by now her time was near, and it seemed that Kalea was telling us as clearly as if it were in English that she was ready now," according to my informant.

Then Kalea walked, on unsteady legs, to her hay shed, the safe haven of comfort in her existence, where she lay down quietly and waited for the vet. She demonstrated no resistance now, either to the sedative or to the blue syringe of Euthenol that took her last breath. Throughout, her eyes were soft, her manner trusting and relaxed. "On the last day of her life," affirmed the horse's owner, "Kalea made the decisions." She also taught those around her a lesson in facing death with dignity and courage.

One veterinarian I know with a small animal practice in New York says she firmly believes that most creatures know when their time is up. They are ready for their departure. That opinion is shared by Connie Howard, who directs our local humane society. She told me how in the middle of a sub-zero Vermont winter her cat had unaccountably gone into hiding under a porch—not a location the animal would ordinarily choose for a midday siesta. Connie had not even realized her pet was sick. But the cat, which had end-stage renal disease, seemed to know exactly what was happening. It was doing its best to die.

Too often, though, people are not ready to take the step that is needed to assist their pets over the threshold. Some want their animals to die "naturally," not realizing that a "natural" death can often be quite painful and prolonged. Then when nature proves too ruthless to be borne they call people like Connie or my veterinary friend for a dose of mercy in the middle of the night.

No one can blame them. Deliberately ending another creature's life is surely one of the hardest decisions we will ever have to make. But regrettably, whether through a failure of nerve, or out of false optimism—hoping for improvement in an incurable condition—many people end up making the process of dying more protracted than it needs to be.

The word "euthanasia" literally means "good death." While death seldom comes at exactly the time or in precisely the fashion we might desire, I believe it can be more than an end to life. Death can be our friend, not our foe. In many cases, euthanasia may be an intelligent choice that provides a painless alternative to unnecessary agony. It can insure that the last moments we share with our pets are tranquil rather than tormented. When it is a compassionate response to suffering, it can become a source of wisdom and a door for growth.

Silently licking his gold-white paw,
Oh gorgeous Celestino, for
God made lovely things, yet
Our lovely cat surpasses them all;
The gold, the iron, the waterfall,
The nut, the peach, apple, granite
Are lovely things to look at, yet,
Our lovely cat surpasses them all.

—"THE CAT" BY JOHN GITTINGS (AGE 8)

7 Bless the Beasts and Children

When I was five years old, my father died. Although I lacked the vocabulary to express it, I was overcome with grief. I remember a lump rising into my throat when other children talked about their dads—a reminder of the incomprehensible fate that had befallen me.

I wish the grownups in my life had taken more time to help me understand what had happened, but in those days many believed that youngsters could be "protected" from disturbing events by building a wall of silence around them. Some offered childish explanations that raised more questions than they answered, like the one offered by my kindergarten teacher, who told me that "God needed your father in heaven more than he did on earth."

As a parent and minister, I've come to believe that the best way to help our children cope with death is by talking about it, frankly and forthrightly. That rule holds whether we are discussing the loss of a person or a pet.

Most children excel at asking questions, if they think it is safe to do so, but adults can sometimes be at a loss for answers, because of their own discomfort or out of a misplaced desire to shelter their offspring from harsh realities.

But the best policy is to be truthful with youngsters, for if they sense their elders evading a topic, they may conclude that it is too scary or worrisome to talk about. Openness, along with gentle reassurance, can allay many of their concerns.

Listen for the "questions behind the questions" children ask. "Why did my cat die?" may be a simple request for information, in which case a brief factual answer is needed. The same question may also cloak unstated issues surrounding guilt and separation (for example, "Did I cause his death? Will I die too?"), which require comfort and emotional support along with understanding. "Why did my pet die?" is unlikely to be a philosophical inquiry, however, unless the child is beyond the primary grades. Younger children are not developmentally ready for such abstract thinking. Be sure of the questions your child is really asking before you attempt to respond.

Whenever possible, stick to the facts. Explain that when a pet dies, it no longer sees, hears, or feels anything. It will not move again or return to life. It does not suffer or sense its surroundings. Avoid using such euphemisms as "we put the pet to sleep," which are likely to leave a child afraid of going to bed at night, confused about the difference between death and normal slumber. If you explain that the pet got sick and died, be sure to add that "getting sick" doesn't necessarily result in death. Otherwise, your child may fear that a cough, a cold, or normal childhood maladies will have grave consequences. You can tell your child honestly that while all living creatures die, it is not something boys or girls need to worry about for a very long time.

Pre-school children lack understanding of the finality or irreversibility of death. They are prone to magical thinking and may wonder if they are somehow responsible for the pet's demise. Slightly older youngsters (ages six to nine) tend to picture death in the form of a ghost or monster and may worry that the same frightening figure who killed their pet will get them too. Because children inhabit a world where make-believe and reality are sometimes difficult to distinguish, it is best to handle the question of death straightforwardly and with concrete answers.

Besides being honest with children, it is important to give them opportunities to express their feelings. For some, the loss of a pet may be a minor matter while for others it is a major trauma. At times it may be difficult to assess how deeply your child is affected, since children typically grieve in brief episodes, with tears quickly passing into apparent indifference, then returning when the child is overtired or out-of-sorts. The safest assumption is that your child is upset, even when outward signs of grief are not readily apparent. Jeanette Jones, a Rutgers University psychologist whose work focuses on child development, says that children typically identify the loss of a pet as the saddest experience of their lives.

It is not unusual for children to mourn the death of "pets" their parents never even knew about—a toad that lived in the neighbor's garden, or some other wild creature with whom the youngster had formed a secret alliance. The director of religious education at our church remembers grieving for such "unofficial" pets as a young girl. She and her friends maintained a small cemetery in a wooded lot near their neighborhood, where they buried worms, dead birds, and other once-living creatures. Although she cannot remember all the details, she can recall that the burial plots were arranged in a crescent formation, and that the children pretended to hold funerals for the animals. Through this kind of play-acting, youngsters can explore their own fears and fantasies about the end of life. Occasionally, such feelings may be too intense to handle and go underground, surfacing only as irritability, clinginess or other forms of "acting out," until the child is strong enough to face them.

That was the case for Elisabeth Kübler-Ross, the researcher who is now famous for her work on death and dying. As a young girl, she had several rabbits that were her childhood pets. She was especially close to these bunnies, because as one of three identical triplets, she often felt as though her parents had little time for her. In fact, the rabbits seemed to be the only ones who could consistently tell Elisabeth apart from her two sisters—since Elisabeth fed them every day, the animals must have noticed whatever slight differences distinguished her from her siblings.

One day, her father told Elisabeth to choose a rabbit to take to the butcher shop, to be slaughtered and trimmed for the family table. Six months later, when he once more grew hungry for roast, the order was repeated, then again repeated. Finally, it the turn of "Blackie," Elisabeth's favorite rabbit. As a last resort, she set the bunny free and begged it to run away, but the animal was so attached to her that it refused to leave. For the final time, Elisabeth carried out the

cruel errand and walked back home with the meat to give
to her mother. The butcher had told her what a shame it
was to have killed the animal. "Blackie" was a female, he
informed her, and in another day or two would have
delivered a whole litter of baby rabbits.

Elisabeth felt such a sense of violation that for decades
she suppressed all memory of the incident. Only as an adult,
having helped hundreds of terminally ill people through the
steps of denial, bargaining, anger, and acceptance, could she
overcome her own denial and acknowledge the rage that
had been buried for so many years. It is a testament to the
resilience of the human spirit that individuals like Kübler-
Ross can not only recover from such frightfulness, but go
on to help and heal others as well.

Fortunately, few children will experience such devastat-
ing losses or have to endure such uncaring parents. But
when a pet dies, many will face all the shock, anger, guilt,
and sadness that accompanies the loss of a loved one, even if
they cannot fully understand death or give names to all their
feelings. Because they grieve intermittently, holding feelings
inside until they feel safe in expressing them, children may
spend many years working through a death, re-experiencing
its impact at successive stages of intellectual and emotional
growth. One should remember that what looms large in
their world may seem trivial to grownups but must be
respected on its own terms.

How differently children can perceive their world
became clear to me just last summer. My own two, who

were six at the time, each had a goldfish. They won the fish
at the county fair by tossing ping-pong balls into empty
fishbowls, insisting on spending their own money despite
my parental mutterings that pets should not be parceled out
as prizes on the midway. I confess that to me the fish were
mostly an annoyance. By the time we had purchased nets,
fishfood, and the other paraphernalia needed, these "free
prizes" had cost me about twenty dollars.

True to my predictions, and in spite of our best efforts
to keep the fish alive, both expired within a few days and
were buried in the back yard beneath small crosses in a
corner by the clothesline. What surprised me was the way
both children continued to ruminate about those fish for
months afterward. The journals my daughter made in school
were adorned with drawings of Rosie (the pet name she
bestows on all her favorite playmates), and in a short autobi-
ographical essay my son wrote almost a year later, the fish
received far more ink than grandparents, Sunday School,
sports, or other items I would have thought more significant. One evening the next spring, I found two delicate
apple blossoms laid upon their graves.

For me, the fish might have been a nuisance, but for my
children, they were apparently symbols for Being itself—
emblems of transience and transcendence for which they
had neither words nor concepts but which cast a powerful
spell upon their minds.

For most children, animals evoke a sense of reverence
and delight. Youngsters may only partly understand their
world, but they sense and appreciate it profoundly.

How do we understand and relate to the child's inner world of nameless worries and half-imagined possibilities? Fortunately, adults can help children cope at their own level in many ways:

Create a ceremony. Involve children in planning a memorial for their pet. Discuss where the animal's remains should be buried. Make an appropriate marker. Decorate the grave. Regardless of age, people need to express love and respect at the time of final parting.

Read a story. Many excellent books on the subject of pet loss have been written for juveniles. Ask your local librarian for suggestions appropriate to your child's age and circumstances.

Write a cinquain to celebrate the pet's life. This is one of the simplest forms of poetry, constructed of five lines, according to the following formula:

First Line—write one noun that names or identifies your subject.

Second Line—add two adjectives that describe the noun.

Third Line—select three verbs that tell what the noun in the first line does.

Fourth Line—think of a short phrase that sums up.

Fifth Line—repeat the word from the first line or choose a synonym for it.

Sammy
sleek, sure-footed
stalks, pounces, misses
there will never be another
Sammy

Draw a picture or make a poster. Invite your child to recapture the qualities he or she most appreciated about the pet. With markers and paints, a youngster can express feelings that are hard to verbalize.

Inform caregivers. Just as for adults, children's sorrow is easier to bear when it is known and shared. Teachers, guidance counselors, and classmates can help provide sympathy to a hurting child.

Finally, if the child wishes, and if such gifts are accepted, donate the pet's leash, bowl, and other equipment in good condition to an animal shelter. It is comforting to know that other creatures will benefit from items that were a part of a cherished pet's life.

For some parents, the temptation may be strong to replace a grieving youngster's pet as soon as possible, but always remember to consult the person most closely involved before making such a decision. Pets should never be given to "surprise" a child who may be unprepared to form another bond. Your child can help you determine if and when the time is right.

As always, straightforward communication is essential. You can share your uncertainties, as well as what you know or surmise about death, but honest questions deserve honest answers. Speaking to children openly and without equivocation about the end of life can help them develop trust in the mystery that surrounds us all.

When despair for the world grows in me
and I wake in the night at the least sound
in fear of what my life and my children's lives may be,
I go and lie down where the wood drake
rests in his beauty on the water, and the great heron feeds.
I come into the peace of wild things
who do not tax their lives with forethought
of grief. I come into the presence of still water.
And I feel above me the day-blind stars
waiting with their light. For a time
I rest in the grace of the world, and am free.

— "THE PEACE OF WILD THINGS"
BY WENDELL BERRY

8 SPEAK TO THE EARTH

When I am feeling bruised or burdened, I often find relief in nature. Walking along the lakeshore near my home, where the water is deep and quiet, can take me beneath the troubled surface of my life to a place that's calm and that restores my soul. The light on the treetops kindles my spirit when it is burning low. When I think the world has been unfair and ask resentfully "Why me?" I find a wordless answer in the out-of-doors. I know I am not unique in this. It's a theme I find repeated in one of the great classics of religious literature, the Biblical book of Job.

This is the story of the way one man copes with misfortune. Through no fault of his own, Job is visited by a series of disasters. First, he loses his cattle and other domestic animals, next his wife and children die, and finally his own health is stolen from him. Formerly a person of wealth and stature, he becomes an object of pity and some scorn among his neighbors. Angrily, Job asks why life has treated him so badly. Where is the justice when such evil befalls an innocent man? "I would speak to the Almighty," Job exclaims, "and I desire to argue my case with God."

Onto this scene come Job's three well-meaning but rather insensitive friends. What do you say to someone who's lost his home, his livelihood, his family, who's covered with boils and sitting on an ashheap, scraping his sores with a broken pot? "I know just how you feel" doesn't seem quite right.

While it is never easy to find words that will bring consolation to one who has suffered a loss, certain errors can be avoided. Comments that give advice ("don't take it so hard"), or discount the pain involved (in the case of a pet, "it was only an animal"), or force a false cheeriness upon the mourner ("it must be God's will," or "it's all for the best") are unlikely to be well-received. Unfortunately, Job's friends make all these mistakes and more. They're of little comfort to a man who needs compassion more than criticism and who needs someone to hold him rather than scold him.

But while Job is mistreated and misunderstood by his neighbors, he continues to protest to God: "Oh, that I knew where I might find him, that I might come even to his seat! I would lay my case before him and fill my mouth with arguments." Job itemizes his complaints and demands that God give some accounting or explanation for this world, which from the human point of view often seems to be rather grossly mismanaged. And Job gets his wish! For the Almighty, the Maker of Heaven of Earth, then makes a grand appearance.

God asks Job to contemplate the marvels of the natural world: the frosty storehouses of snow and hail, the hidden sources of the wind and rain, the high-vaulting courses of clouds and constellations overhead. Above all, God invites Job to consider the astonishing members of the animal kingdom: the mountain goat, the wild ass and ostrich that roam freely over their domain, the ox and stallion in their might, the crocodile and hippopotamus so fierce and heedless of danger. "Is it by your wisdom that the hawk soars, and spreads his wings toward the south?" God challenges Job. "Is it at your command that the eagle mounts up and makes his nest on high?"

The closing chapters of the book of Job contain some of the world's most evocative religious verse, stunning the reader with images of a world that is wild and free, alive with the energy of creation. Thus Job is answered, but not in the way he expected. He does not receive a redress for his grievances or a logical reply to his arguments. Instead, he is swept away by a spiritual experience. "I had heard of thee by the hearing of the ear," Job says to God in the final chapter of the book, "but now my eye sees thee." Not through rational demonstration, but rather by means of a profound perceptual shift, Job regains an appreciation for the poetry of life.

Healing may be as close as the ground beneath our feet. That, it seems to me, is one lesson to be learned from the book of Job. No one, of course, can manufacture an awareness of the sacred. But like Job, we can look upward toward the Pleiades, or Orion, or the Great Bear with her children, and perhaps gain a glimmering of the infinite. Standing by the sea, we sense forces that are vast and unsearchable, and we may even feel our own difficulties diminish by contrast. Studies have shown that when patients in the hospital have a window in their room where

they can see trees and grass and birds, rather than asphalt
and bricks and concrete, they get well sooner. The natural
world holds recuperative properties that can mend our
bodies as well as hearts and minds.

I was reminded of this when I gathered some years ago
with a group of other men and women who were training
to care for the bereaved and dying as volunteers in our
local hospice program. The focus of the day was spirituality,
and the instructor introduced it by asking each of us to
respond to the question "What makes your spirit soar?"
There were about twenty people present—Quakers, Catholics,
Jews, and some with no particular religious affiliation. But
despite the diversity in the room, there was one thing we
all had in common. Everyone found renewal in nature.
Gazing into the golds of a setting sun, or hiking above the
tree line where the vistas stretch for miles, stirred something profound in all of us. Some found exaltation in other
places, too—in music or silence, in scripture or service. But
without exception, we were inspired and uplifted by the
power of earth and sea and sky. As we read in the book of Job:

> Ask now the beasts, and they shall teach thee;
> And the fowls of the air, and they shall teach thee;
> Or speak to the earth, and it shall teach thee,
>> and the fishes of the earth shall
>> declare unto thee;
> Who knoweth not that in all these
>> That the hand of God hath wrought this?
> In whose hand is the soul of every living thing. . . .

Every creature embodies a divine principle, and one of the reasons we treasure our pets is that they remind us of the miracle of life. But even when they are gone, the world remains awesome in its ability to teach and transform us.

Has life lost its melody? Take time to sit and listen to the music of a forest stream. Are you dejected? Pay attention to what the bluejay says to the mountain. If we are receptive, the beings who share our living planet can bring balm to our distress. They may not answer the question, "Why?" at least not in words. But as on eagle's wings, they can lift us above discouragement.

Warm summer sun, shine kindly here;
Warm western wind, blow softly here;
Green sod above, lie light, lie light—
Good-night, dear heart, good-night, good-night.

—ROBERT RICHARDSON (ADAPTED BY MARK TWAIN)

9 Rest in Peace

Alongside the old-fashioned New England meetinghouse where our congregation worships each week is a small garden, where the ashes of our departed members lie in rest. No permanent markers are visible there. Only memories inhabit the area. No urns or other lasting containers are under the surface, either. The remains are allowed to go back to the earth. I don't mind the lack of marble head-stones or granite monuments, for unlike stone, the things that make life precious, including love and companionship, are fragile and perishable. But like the flowers that adorn our garden, they can bloom again and again.

People have buried their dead like this from time out of mind. Such customs are at least as old as humankind, and perhaps even older, since other species appear to have kindred rites. Elephants are known to cover the bodies of their fallen comrades with soil and brush in much the same way that we bury our friends and family members when they die. Badgers have been reported to do the same for their mates, sometimes circling the grave with plaintive moans and whimpers. For whatever reason—to find closure, to offer dignity to the dead, or to satisfy some primordial need we ourselves only partially understand—

human beings share with animals in this impulse to return the physical remnants of the departed to the ground from which they came.

Some of the oldest human burials contain the remains of other creatures. One of these, for example, took place in northern Israel, where archaeologists discovered two skeletons that had been laid side by side: an elderly human being and a puppy just a few months old. The pair had been buried together approximately twelve thousand years ago. Touchingly, the person's hand had been carefully placed to rest upon the dog's shoulder, as if petting or protecting it. One wonders: was the animal killed deliberately, or was this a case where dog or master had followed the other to the grave? In any event, the gesture revealed by the exhumation seemed to express the timeless connection between person and pet, a relationship that outlasts even death.

According to Valerie Porter in her book *Faithful Companions,* cemeteries for dogs were quite common among the ancient Egyptians, who idolized the animals. Given special protection by Egyptian law, dogs were frequently appointed guardians of temples and often embalmed after death. The god Anubis, who guarded the portals of the netherworld and escorted souls on their last journey, was envisioned as a dog- or jackal-headed deity, a mythic association that presumably gave his more mundane canine cousins added appeal. But one imagines that, even in a culture where animals were revered as supernatural entities, people may have felt a down-to-earth affection for their pets. Near the Great Pyramid of Cheops, a stone slab carries an inscription from

the Pharoah to his dog indicating the personal attention
given to these animals:

> The dog was guard of His Majesty.
> Abuwityuw was his name. His Majesty
> ordered that he be buried ceremonially, that
> he be given a coffin from the royal treasury,
> fine linen in great quantity, and incense.

Cats were equally valued, and after their death great efforts
were made to preserve their bodies through the process of
mummification. After being embalmed and placed in a coffin,
cats were commonly buried in sections of land along the
Nile reserved especially for that purpose. Human family
members who lost their pets typically shaved their eyebrows
as a sign of mourning.

Archaeologists recently discovered in the Middle East
another graveyard for dogs tentatively dating back to 450
B.C.E. All the animals in the burial ground seem to have
died of natural causes; a few showed traces of arthritis. To
judge from skeletal remains, the dogs were of the greyhound
type, and each was buried individually with great care.
Apparently, these were sporting hounds, esteemed by the
aristocracy. The humbler classes may well have honored
their own animals with similar burials but without such
enduring monuments.

It seems that the need to find a suitable resting place for
our animal companions is both old and deep-seated. Burials
do have a practical aspect, and putting bodies in the ground
disposes of them permanently and hygienically. But the
practice may also spring from an intuition about the nature

of grieving: soil must be turned and broken before new life can take root. In the modern world of America and Europe, special cemeteries for pets have existed for more than a hundred years.

A simple backyard burial may be suitable for small animals. One girl who was particularly upset by the death of her dog—she had become hysterical and fainted on hearing the news—reported that she had been especially helped by her boyfriend, who insisted that she dig the grave herself and place the dog's body into the ground with her own hands. After filling the grave, she placed on it a stone bearing the inscription "Here Lies Love." It was the physical act of caring for her dog's body, a parting gesture of devotion, that enabled her to bear up under very difficult circumstances.

Handling the body oneself can reinforce the finality of death and makes the loss more tangible. Still, some may employ the services of a commercial pet cemetery or look to their veterinarian or a local humane society to assist with a cremation. Arrangements differ, but the impulse to celebrate the continuity of life even in the presence of death remains the same. Writing of her cat's death in the *New York Times,* author Mary Cantwell speaks to this common need to ritualize our parting:

> This spring, when the ground is no longer frozen and the animal mortuary delivers the little box, I will take Calypso's ashes to the country and bury them under a beach plum bush. Our first cat is interred there, along with my older daughter's kitten.

A stone cat is curled under the branches. A
garden ornament that was a gift from a
friend, it acts as a headstone. The burial will
involve a small ritual—"Goodbye, Calypso,"
maybe, and a farewell toast—and if I look
foolish, I don't care. Ceremony is one of the
crutches I use to get through life.

But ceremony is more than a crutch. Rituals are the means
we use to hallow time. They mark certain moments as being
"momentous" rather than merely momentary in their
import and significance.

It would be a mistake to assume that such rites of passage
must be grim or longfaced. You can be serious without being
somber. One friend of mine, for example, assembled a small
congregation of toy animals to attend the burial of a para-
keet. Epitaphs may also be whimsical: "She never knew she
was a cat." Such farewells may sound frivolous, but laughter
and tears are close cousins. And the purpose of a memorial is
not to dwell on life's unpleasantness but to commemorate
the qualities that make it glad as well as poignant.

When a pet is buried, the interment is usually per-
formed with much less pomp and circumstance than is the
case with human commitals. Most people seem to like an
informal leavetaking and assume an idiosyncratic approach
to their final partings, but the good-byes are no less genuine
for that. In an article titled "Best Damm Dog We Ever
Had," Richard Meyer and David Gradwolh contrast the San
Francisco National Cemetery, a military gravesite, with the
neighboring Presidio Pet Cemetery, where the animals of

army personnel are interred. In one, uniform white markers stand aligned in orderly but rather sterile procession. In the other, homemade headstones in cheerful disarray are decorated with folk art flourishes: living plants and artificial flowers, helium balloons and colored ribbons, weathering photographs of dogs and cats along with packets of "Hearty Chews." Inscriptions have a homespun integrity, like the one for Jane, a Chinese Water Dragon:

> She lived a full life of 10 years. She was the
> greatest lizard I ever knew and will be greatly
> missed by Emily her owner and friends Randall,
> Poncho, Nellie, Mr. Iguana, Lucy Rabbit and
> the many others who knew and loved her.

Unlike their human counterparts, these memorials are anything but restrained. They seem playful by contrast. But while no twenty-one gun salutes, flag-draped coffins, or brass bands marked their passing, these animals could truly be said to have been buried with full honors.

When the day finally comes for me to lay my own dog's ashes in the ground, I know I will want to sing a round of "Auld Lang Syne" and spend some time looking through our photo albums, where my dog's pictures will always reside along with the rest of our treasured family snapshots. I know I will cry, and I may even chuckle once or twice when I recall the day he ate the drapes, but the pictures will remind me that wherever their bodies may lie—beneath plum or cherry, under granite markers, or scattered to the winds—our animals can rest in peace. Their memories are secure within our hearts.

Apprehend God in all things,
for God is in all things.
Every single creature is full of God
and is a book about God.
Every creature is a word of God.

— MEISTER ECKHART

10   Healing Words

I have delivered many eulogies in my years of ministry. One of the most difficult, and one of the most healing, was for my own grandfather. Because we were so close, I felt overwhelmed with emotion. I had to pause at several points during his memorial service before I could continue speaking. But while I was on the verge of weeping, I also felt something strangely like euphoria. I experienced a profound sense of gratitude and joy for the relationship we had shared. From that episode, I learned how transforming the spoken word can be. By giving voice to the love inside us, we bring it alive and give it power—a power that is even stronger than death.

I usually counsel those who are grieving to employ the power of words by writing a eulogy for the one they love. The term itself means "good words," for a eulogy attempts to sum up the qualities that made another person memorable and worthy of our care. In the case of an animal, a eulogy could take the form of a letter, poem, or memoir that reflects on the traits that made that creature most endearing or stamped it with a special personality.

Of course, words are never adequate to summarize another's life. A three-dimensional being can never be reduced to the two-dimensional surface of a written page. But in attempting to articulate what made an animal lovable and unique, we may discover subtleties that were previously unspoken or not so richly appreciated. I have written dozens of eulogies in my time, and it is always a difficult task, but when I succeed in capturing the essence of one who has died, it is one of the most satisfying things I do in my capacity as a clergyman—hard work but rewarding. I know my words have made a difference.

Committing one's words to paper has several virtues. Writing requires active recollection, which stirs the well of memory. At the same time it creates a lasting keepsake for the future, which along with photos, pawprints, and other mementos will only grow more valuable as the years go by. Reading the words aloud also has a purpose. It heightens their impact, and by calling on the senses (shaping the syllable on the tongue, hearing the timbre of one's own voice sound upon the ear) impresses their meaning upon the awareness.

Every eulogy has a beginning, middle, and end, and in this respect it resembles life itself. The process of writing forces us to focus on the main storyline and look for the significant detail. What were the highlights of the life that is being commemorated? What difference did this animal make in our lives? Turning experience into story form is one of the ways we make sense of our lives and give meaning to existence. And bringing our stories to conclusion can help us find closure when faced with death. The living manuscript that was once a work-in-progress has come to a definitive end. Not only is a life over, a narrative has reached completion.

Many famous writers have penned paeans to their pets, including D.H. Lawrence ("Rex"), James Thurber ("Snapshot of a Dog"), May Sarton (*The Fur Person*), and E.B. White (whose obituary for his dog Daisy concludes, "she died sniffing life, and enjoying it"). But one need not be a best-selling author or a master stylist to create a meaningful *in memoriam*.

My fellow minister the Reverend Elizabeth Tarbox wrote for her pet the following thoughtful eulogy, which expresses both the sadness and the mood of reflection that can descend when a good friend dies. I have admired her work for many years, and so I clipped this piece from her church newsletter as soon as I saw it, for it shows how much life can be evoked in a few well-chosen words:

> Natalie was a gold-and-white guinea pig, with full lips and an overstated stomach. She shared her life with us, accepted our love and care, nibbled daintily on spinach and dande-lion, and swooned over the very smell of strawberries. Natalie cherished her mate, Frank, and let us stroke their babies, and forgave us when we gave the babies away.
>
> When Natalie got sick we took her to the veterinarian and were told she would not get well again, so we made that choice which we human animals have granted our-selves and asked the doctor to put her to sleep. But Natalie didn't sleep. She lay in my lap and quivered and sighed and the life that

she had so generously shared with us left her little round body and she was dead.

And I thought, how curious it is that this small animal should move me so, that this little life whose whole span had been but five years should make me wrestle with my conscience about the rights of humans to have charge over animals; how strange that this lifeless furry creature with the now still body should bring me to tears.

I had personified a guinea pig. I had granted her a place and dignity in my home. Somehow by my love I had elevated her to something more than a species of rodent. But she in turn had dignified me by accepting my care. She had brought beauty into our home, and had stirred in me emotions I am glad to have: love and the desire to nurture. She had trusted me and thereby had made me trustworthy.

It is remarkable how such a diminutive creature can summon our spirits toward the immensities. But perhaps it is true that the smaller another being is or the more dependent it is, the bigger our corresponding responsibilities become. Because they are innocent, animals can help us to become wise. To the extent that they are carefree, they may enable us to become more caring.

As a parent, I know that having children is one of the things that has helped me to become more grown up; as a pet owner, I think that caring for an animal is one of the things that has let me become more human. The Reverend Tarbox concludes her tribute to Natalie with the following prayer, which might be spoken for every living creature:

Great God make us friends of the animals. Make us responsible co-inhabitants with them of this fruitful planet. In our dealings with animals, may we be generous; may we exercise our power with compassion and avoid brutality; may we never debase them; may we never use their flesh or their skins wastefully to enhance our appearance; may we respect their right to a good life in their own habitat. In our dealings with animals may we remember that all life is mysterious and precious and God-given and that we are honored and blessed by their presence among us.

Can we say Amen? Through words like these, we affirm the sanctity of life, even in the presence of death. We express our gratitude for the gift of our time on earth. As the mystical writer Meister Eckhart reminded us, if the only prayer we ever said were "Thank You," that would be enough.

Words are creative. They can motivate, chasten, consecrate, and reconcile. They not only describe reality, they can change it as well. We all know that words have the ability to hurt. Why shouldn't they also have the capacity to heal and transform our world? When uttered with sincerity, our words may bring us closer to a place of wholeness and peace.

Old Blue died and he died so hard,
Shook the ground in my back yard.
Dug his grave with a silver spade,
Lowered him down with links of chain.
With every link I did call his name:
Here, Blue, you good dog you.
Here, Blue, I'm a coming too!

— AMERICAN FOLKSONG

11 THE ETERNAL QUESTION

A living creature possesses an indefinable but unmistakable presence that distinguishes it from a dead one. The contrast is noticeable, even before the body has had time to grow cold. Robbie Kahn, a sociologist who teaches at the University of Vermont, told me how she personally discovered what a difference a single breath can make as she shared the last moments of her dog Sarah's life. Robbie sat on the floor next to her companion. The dog drew air into its lungs quietly, in a slightly watery tone, and the interval between each exhalation grew longer. Then the final breath left the dog's body.

The change in the room was instantaneous and almost palpable. Where there were two beings present a heartbeat earlier, now there was only one. "Later," recalled Robbie, "I would remember that moment and wonder, as I still wonder, where could she have gone so suddenly, how could she be so suddenly gone?" Does the spirit simply vanish at the instant of death or somehow take flight? People have puzzled about this mystery for thousands of years.

The question of whether animals survive death, like the conundrum of human immortality, is probably unanswerable. When Koko, a lowland gorilla who has learned to converse in American Sign Language, was asked the question, "Where do gorillas go when they die?" she responded to her trainer with the gestures "*comfortable / hole* (the sign for a hole in the ground) / *bye* (touching fingers to lips as if kissing a person good-bye)." Her answer suggests that other species have given some thought to what might lie beyond this world, and it is humbling to realize that Koko's ideas about the afterlife are probably as good as yours or mine.

Yet many of us would agree that heaven—however we conceive it—would be a paltry place without the animals who keep us company and provide so many of life's lighter moments. A paradise with "No Pets Allowed" posted over the pearly gates would hardly be an attractive destination.

Various religious traditions have commented upon this problem. The only writer of the Bible who directly addresses the issue is Ecclesiastes, who expresses a gentle agnosticism on this, as on so many other riddles of existence:

> For the fate of humans and the fate of
> animals is the same; as one dies, so dies the
> other. . . . Who knows whether the human
> spirit goes upward and the spirit of the
> animals goes downward to the earth?

What happens to people and other living beings when they die is a matter of faith, on which people may differ according to their own beliefs. My own sympathies are with the woman who, when she was asked whether she wished to be buried or cremated upon her demise, replied simply, "Surprise me!"

Many eastern traditions hold elaborate theories of the transmigration of souls from animal to human and back again. The *Jataka Tales*, for instance, tell of the Buddha's previous incarnations in animal form, as antelope, monkey, elephant, dog, peacock, and a myriad of other creatures. Throughout these stories, the animals act as teachers and exemplars to the human characters, as in the fable of the unselfish stag that saves the life of a king who once hunted him. "I myself was the stag," the Buddha tells his listeners. In this tradition, animals, like their human counterparts, are capable of enlightenment and liberation.

Christianity in the main denies that other species share in the hope of an afterlife, but a few raised dissenting voices. John Wesley, the founder of Methodism, was convinced he would see his horse in heaven. The popular theologian C.S. Lewis also refused to exclude other creatures from eternity, speculating somewhat fiendishly that a mosquito's experience of paradise might very well include tormenting human sinners in hell!

In Judaism, redemption is primarily understood in communal terms rather than as individual survival beyond the grave. But the Hebrew scriptures contain numerous indications that God's mercy extends to all living things. "Every beast of the forest is mine," saith the Lord. And again, "I know all the fowls of the mountains; and the wild beasts of the field are mine." The messianic vision of *shalom* is of a world restored to its original unity, where lion and lamb lie down together and a little child shall lead them.

In light of such diversity of opinion, it might be unwise to be dogmatic. Surely, life after death is one topic on which people of sincere faith and good will may reasonably disagree. Still, some are convinced that animals have a spirit that does survive bodily cessation. Stories of dogs and cats who refuse to "give up the ghost" are legion.

In *Memories,* a fine tribute to his spaniel Chris, the author John Galsworthy relates one such inexplicable incident. It was at the dark end of December, and the author's wife was in a reflective mood when she became aware of the dog's black body passing round the room to take his place at his old, accustomed spot under the table. It was an apparition, for the animal had died some time before. She saw the dog clearly, heard the tap-tapping of his paws and toenails scratching across the floor, even felt his warmth brush her skirt as he sidled in front of her and pressed briefly against her with his weight. Then something broke the spell—a sound or some other distraction momentarily claimed her attention—and as her consciousness returned to the room, very slowly the dog disappeared.

Such experiences may be more common than many people realize. One study of bereavement indicated that as many as one in six of those who lose a pet may continue to hear the animal in the house or sense its presence in other ways after death. Grief counselors are well aware that in cases of human loss, people often experience "visitations" of their departed loved ones. The same seems to be true when pets die.

Explanations vary. Maybe the spirit actually does survive in a form that can make itself felt and known. Or perhaps the mourner finds it so difficult to believe the animal has actually died that the mind play tricks on itself. A dog barking in the distance may sound unmistakably like a long-lost friend; a noisy branch scraping the side of the house can be confused for a beloved pet scratching at the door. The unconscious can, after all, be extremely creative. Some people dream about their pets after they have passed on, and at times the images can be very vivid as well as reassuring. The animal we remember as old and sick may appear once more as healthy and vigorous. A part of our psyche seems to be telling us not to worry about death or what lies beyond this world. There may be wisdom in such messages from the subconscious.

How should we regard the passing of life to death? How much do we dare to hope? Galsworthy's thoughts on this matter seem so sensible that they deserve quotation. Writing of his dog Chris, he reflects on the question of whether animals know, as we do, that their time must come.

Yes, they know, at rare moments. No other way can I interpret those pauses of his latter life, when, propped on his forefeet, he would sit for long minutes quite motion-less—his head drooped, utterly withdrawn; then turn those eyes of his and look at me. That look said more plainly that all words could: "Yes, I know that I must go!" If *we* have spirits that persist—*they* have. If *we*

know after our departure, who we were—
they do. No one, I think, who really longs for
truth, can ever glibly say which it will be for
dog and man—persistence or extinction of
our consciousness. There is but one thing
certain—the childishness of fretting over that
eternal question.

As night follows day, life and whatever waits beyond will
unfold just as the universe has decreed. "Whichever it be,
it must be right," as Galsworthy concludes, "the only possible thing."

God made all the creatures and them our love and our fear,
To give sign, we and they are his children, one family here.

— ROBERT BROWNING

12 THE CONTINUUM OF LIFE

Mortality nudges into our awareness at different points in our lives. Sometimes it strikes like a fist, at others it brushes alongside with the merest touch. It tapped me on the shoulder several years ago, about the time my wife and I were trying to have children.

Because of a serious illness in my youth, I had to take various medicines on a daily and ongoing basis. I was grateful for these drugs, which literally saved my life. But it was ironic when my physicians told me that I might never be able to father offspring. Tests showed that as a side effect of the medication I had become almost completely infertile.

The news created a crisis of meaning for me. What was the point of living, I asked, if one day I would vanish from the earth and leave no progeny? Every trace of me would disappear. Each morning I walked to a small park near our home, where I would sit and think about these questions. Usually my dog, who was just a puppy then, would come along.

As I watched him run and gambol it occurred to me that life is a continuum. Every part is connected. The dog frisking on the grass, the swallows swooping low over the field in search of insects, the ripening blackberries—each living thing is vital to the well-being of the whole. My own life would end someday, I realized, but the important thing was that life itself would continue. Whatever was essential would be preserved.

My dog is older now, and so am I. At eleven, he walks more slowly because of the fatty tumors under his joints. He has also had to adjust to the two children that have been added to our household, one who is adopted and one who is not. Equally enamored with both of my children, I wonder at my earlier obsession with perpetuating my own personal strand of DNA. Having a family, I understand now, is more about sharing love than sharing genes.

Doctors are sometimes wrong, I found out. Miracles do happen. Vets can be mistaken, too, like the one who told me that my dog would not likely last the winter. When he said that, it was no tickle in the ribs. His prediction felt more like a jab in the solar plexus. But that was two years ago, and with the help of two aspirins a day, my dog is still game to chase a squirrel or go wading in the lake.

But doctors and veterinarians are right in their long-term prognosis. For all of us, human and otherwise, life is a condition that is a hundred percent fatal. When the blow finally falls and Chinook dies, I may stagger a bit. Intellectually, I know he may not last much longer, but emotionally, I will probably be completely unprepared, like most others, for the *coup de grace*. For some reason, though, death no longer frightens me as it once did. It too is part of the continuum.

I am reminded of a dream I once had. In the dream, I am driving down a solitary road. Dense forest lies on either side of the highway. Suddenly, a deer emerges from the thicket and leaps into the roadway, where it stands momentarily illuminated in the bright sunshine. Where I had thought myself alone, I now find that I am regarded by an Other, exchanging looks that combine amazement and rapt attention. Then, as quickly as it appeared, the deer disappears, bounding into the dark shade of the woods on the other side of the road.

That deer is followed by another, which also appears and disappears, and then another, which likewise materializes and vanishes. Each one evokes, for me, the same surge of delight. Time stands still as the animals, one by one, leap into sight. I seem to be praying, not with my voice but with my entire body, whose molecules are shouting "Yes!" and "More!" Though different individuals, all the deer contain the same marvelous essence of Otherness.

The meaning of the dream was at once apparent to me. It was about life and death, birth and rebirth. For life disappears and reappears under diverse disguises. It reveals itself for a single flashing, startling instant before returning to the impenetrable darkness from which it came. But through all its many manifestions, there endures something worthy of our wonder and awe.

The same stream flows in everyone. My old, stiff-legged dog is not the same as the romping puppy I learned to love all those years ago, though he seems no less beautiful to me. My adopted son is not the same as my biological daughter, yet I see something of myself reflected in both of them. In each child and every creature, there is a presence that awakens what is most tender and ardent in ourselves.

It is always there, ready to be rediscovered, even when we seem to lose sight of it. Having run beyond our vision, the object of our dreams will spring back into view, going and coming within the continuum of life.

Next to the encounter of death in our own bodies, the most sensible calamity to an honest man is the death of a friend. The comfort of having a friend may be taken away, but not that of having had one. Shall a man bury his friendship with his friend?

— SENECA

13 TODAY AND TOMORROW

The past cannot be changed and can never be recreated. Yesterday is a tale that has already been told. But today and tomorrow are still before us, waiting to be realized. They are the framework in which we have to live.

What can we do when an animal companion dies? Staying busy is not a bad idea. Volunteers are always needed at animal welfare organizations, if you seek an outlet for your energy. Donations made in the memory of a pet are always welcome, too. But no amount of money can bring back the dead, and no act of ours can alter what might have been. The human condition is tragic in this sense: we are ephemeral, transitory beings, and there is nothing we can do about it. If we fail to realize that, the urge to "stay busy" can devolve from purposeful engagement to frantic activity. It takes on a compulsive quality and becomes a tactic for avoiding our own feelings of loss and fragility when what is needed is to meet them head on. We cannot avoid the darkness or find a way around it. Instead, we must pass through it to reach the light.

But if the things that we can *do* are limited, the things that we can *be* are manifold: patient, accepting, and compassionate with ourselves, sensitive to the currents of sympathy that surround us, and hopeful that even in the midst of sorrow the future will open new possibilities for life. Inside each one of us is a center that is affirming rather than negating, expansive rather than constricting. Finding that center and holding to it can help us live creatively even when the world round about seems chaotic and confused.

Grieving takes time, and mourning sticks to no prescribed schedule. While it will not happen instantly or immediately, the sadness we feel from losing a pet can gradually diminish while warm and funny memories remain and grow richer in our minds. We recall good times we shared. Eventually, we can look back calmly on the years gone by—never without a tinge of sorrow, but with a powerful feeling of gratitude for a wonderful friendship. We know how blessed we have been to love and be loved, even if only for a short interlude.

But while time is required, the mere passage of hours is not enough to resolve a grief. It is also important to make time our ally, working with it rather than against it as it carries us toward new cycles of life. How can we cooperate with time, the great healer, and let it perform its task?

For today and tomorrow, we can take care of our bodies. We can eat properly, exercise regularly, and sleep at regular intervals. We can visit a physician when needed. We can allow the strength and lifegiving force that resides in flesh, muscle, nerve, and bone to restore us to vitality.

For today and tomorrow, we can embrace our feelings. We can ask for support from family and friends. We can practice forgiveness with ourselves and others. We can realize that in our struggle to face loss we are not alone.

For today and tomorrow, we can accept our own unique and unrepeatable lifespan. We can become aware of the opportunities for enjoyment and camaraderie that each day holds. We can let go of unwanted fears and fixations. We can let the past enrich us rather than enthrall us.

For today and tomorrow, we can pay attention to nature. We can sense our connection to a world that is dynamic and alive. We can breathe deeply and walk reverently. We can notice the beauty of clouds and leaves and other creatures. We can make friends with the earth, from which we are born and to which we ultimately return. We can awaken to the wonders that exist above our heads and beneath our feet.

For today and tomorrow, we can cultivate inwardness. We can take time for prayer, meditation, and thoughtful reflection. We can practice stillness. We can write and journal to bring the unspoken and inarticulate into conscious awareness. We can let ourselves become channels for the universal spirit. We can be open to the guidance of dreams and inner visions.

For today and tomorrow, we can invoke the presence of the sacred. We can worship in church, synagogue, temple, or mosque, or within the chambers of our own being. We can receive the teachings of ancient scriptures, which speak of the Eternal within a world of change, and we can hold to the truth within ourselves. We can have faith that in spite of death and parting, all is in the hands of goodness and mercy.

Finally, we can avoid making life more complicated than it has to be. Not long ago, when I happened to be feeling particularly glum, I shared my mood with my daughter and asked if she had any good cures for the blues. "If you're feeling sad," she suggested with grade-school simplicity, "why not do some things that you think are fun?" It was sound advice, I felt, and I pass it on to you.

Healing will happen, if we let it, perhaps not this day or the next, but eventually. What is required is to persevere, "one day at a time," or as one member of my congregation says who likes to plan ahead, two days at a time. If we can manage to be just a little kinder, more mindful, and in closer touch with our own healthy center—for today and tomorrow—we can trust in life to work its magic cure.

The rugged old Norsemen spoke of death as Heimgang—home-going. So the snow flowers go home when they melt and flow to the sea, and the rock-ferns, after unrolling their fronds to the light and beautifying the rocks, roll them up close again in autumn and blend with the soil. Myriads of rejoicing living creatures, daily, hourly, perhaps every moment sink into death's arms, dust to dust, spirit to spirit. . . .

— JOHN MUIR

14 A Final Gift

A member of my church invited me to bring the children down to her farm this spring to see the baby lambs. We set out on a sunny Sunday afternoon near the end of March and had only a short drive on unpaved roads to reach her home, with beautiful views of the neighboring hills. In Vermont, you are never far from the countryside.

There were seventeen lambs, and three of the ewes were still pregnant. A shaggy ram with massive curling horns was tethered safely in the yard, regarding us with a proprietary stare from his great yellow eyes as we entered the animals' enclosure. None of the lambs was more than three weeks old, but all were exuberant: climbing up the small mountains of hay that had been placed there to nourish them, sliding down or being shoved aside by their brothers and sisters, then bounding once again toward the summit in an apparent effort to defy the laws of gravity. Their capers were contagious and made the children skip. Although there was still a foot of snow on the ground and we were soon heading indoors to get warm, the season of rebirth had clearly arrived.

One of the lambs was named "Hope." The little creature had been delivered strong and healthy shortly after another, less fortunate, that arrived stillborn. While sad, such casualties are part of the landscape for country people, who understand that death is a part of life, as much as gestation, growth, and aging. It is only in modern, technological societies that death appears as a stranger, fearsome because so unfamiliar in our controlled and humanly contrived environment.

For many of us who live in cities and suburbs, a family pet may be our closest living link to the cycles of nature. We may no longer be able to see lambing in the spring; we may have to strain to hear the chorus of geese flying south in the fall, but through the creatures who share our homes we can still experience some of the wonderment of living. Our animal companions remain part of a natural order where beginnings and endings are woven inextricably in a single garment of creation.

Whether we are seeing a kitten opening its eyes for the very first time or watching the last breath slowly leaving the frame of an old and trusted dog, we are witnessing two sides of the same marvelous event. From out of the infinite realm of possibility, a never-to-be repeated creature comes into being, looks out briefly on the universe, passes its life force along to coming generations, then rejoins the undifferentiated vastness from which it emerged. For millions of years, this has been the pattern of life as it perpetuates itself and evolves.

Birth and Death: could any of us invent a more beautiful way to enter this world or devise a more natural route for leaving it at the end? Animals enrich our lives in countless ways, with their playfulness, their tranquility, their constancy, and their love. If they can help us remember that death is not our enemy but simply one more moment in the world's endless process of becoming, dissolution, and renewal, they will have imparted a final gift.

SPECIAL SECTION

A selection of readings on life and death,
with resources for commemorating
the lives of our animal companions.

CREATING YOUR OWN CEREMONY

When a member of my congregation dies, I usually offer the surviving members of the family a book of readings—poems, prayers, and meditations that can help them to reflect quietly on life's final episode. It helps them to gather their thoughts. It invites them to look inward at a time when the outer world may feel unmanageable or over-whelming. It connects them with a spiritual heritage in which loss is an inevitable feature of human experience but in which love is also real and abiding.

The following collection of readings are especially intended for those who have lost a pet. The authors included here span many centuries, from ancient Rome to modern America. They represent a range of religious perspectives, from Navajo to Hindu to Christian. Some of the readings are tributes to departed companions. Others speak to the role animals play in our lives, or to the universals of resignation and hope. Because they are so varied, you will undoubtedly find some more significant than others. But knowing that people in every time and place have faced death and, out of their own differing traditions, found reasons to trust in life, instills confidence.

You may wish to incorporate readings that seem especially appropriate into a service of commemoration for your pet. Such a celebration might be held at home, at the grave site, or in a park where the ashes are to be scattered. If an animal's remains are unavailable for an interment, or if you want to keep them, you might consider planting a tree or some flowers in a quiet corner, to symbolize our connection with the earth, which is the source of life and rebirth. Some people place a marker outdoors in memory of their companions, or buy a special frame for their favorite photograph to hang indoors. An example of one family's ritual of leavetaking that might be used as a model in creating your own ceremony can be found at the conclusion of this section.

A memorial can be solitary, or friends and family members may also be gathered in farewell. In some cases, not everyone who actually cared for a pet can be present when the animal dies. Children who grew up with the animal may be away at college, for instance. Coming to terms with the death may be especially difficult for those who lack the chance to say a personal goodbye. A memorial that is held at some later point, when all who are affected by the loss are reassembled, can offer everyone concerned an opportunity to grieve and support each other in healing.

Most memorials I conduct include a period of silence, permitting participants to be alone with their thoughts, as well as a brief time for sharing, when those present are invited to recall their best and most loving memories. If you would like to offer a eulogy, this is the time. A reading at the beginning of the service and a prayer at the end can open and close such simple ceremonies, invoking a sense of reverence and gratitude and setting apart these few minutes of affectionate tribute as sacred time. You will find words here for both ingathering and benediction. A typical ceremony might include the following elements:

Centering Ourselves: Begin with a meditation that helps you connect with the source of your own being. Some might choose a passage from Saint Francis, while others may select one from the Bhagavad-Gita, or from another spiritual tradition represented here. Turn to whatever truth you find lifegiving and dependable. Whether you name the object of your faith God, the Great Spirit, or Mother Earth, this reality provides the context in which all creatures live and breathe and holds out the promise of renewal.

Acknowledging Our Loss: Give expression to the sorrow that accompanies the death of a beloved companion. Name your pain. Several readings included here convey the mood of bleakness and desolation that grief can bring. A ceremony of remembrance should be one occasion when we have permission to weep and vent our sadness.

Honoring Our Memories: While a memorial service offers a chance to mourn, it should also offer the opportunity to give thanks. Remember everything that was outstanding, praiseworthy, or just plain peculiar about your pet. Poems like the youthful verse that John Gittings wrote for his cat Celestino, which appears at the beginning of chapter seven, or prayers like George Appleton's that you will find later in this section, celebrate the beauty we find in other creatures. Use a poem or prayer from this book, or write one of your own, that gives voice to your feelings of thanksgiving.

Expressing Our Hope: Most memorials I conduct end with an affirmation of the life ahead. Ideally, the experience of loss inspires us to care for each other and to value each day we are given: to be kinder with ourselves and more appreciative of the world around us. You may also want to share your hopes for the future. How will you be changed as a result of the time you shared with your animal companion? In what ways would you like to live differently, or more intentionally, in years to come?

In addition to planning a memorial, you may also want to remember your pet at regular intervals after the animal's death. If your companion was ten years old, for example, you might light a candle at the dinner table for ten days following the loss. You could choose one of the readings included here to accompany such a ritual. Take a moment to recollect where you were, and what you were doing, during each of those years you spent together. Setting aside a prescribed period for grieving—a few minutes every morning or evening for a week or two following the death—can insure that you have at least a portion of each day reserved for time you need to mourn. Observing anniversaries, after a month has passed or yearly on the date of your animal's death, is also important for many people.

Making meaning out of life, including life's finale, is the only way to transform grief into wisdom. Finding a purpose to existence is the only thing that keeps our suffering from being pointless. Moving beyond brokenness means integrating loss into a wider framework of understanding that can embrace both birth and death as parts of a larger whole. Meaning, purpose, and understanding can be discovered only within ourselves. Fortunately, the poets and philosophers of many ages and cultures are ready to help us in our quest.

READINGS AND POEMS YOU CAN USE

Thou hast made the moon to measure the year
and taught the sun where to set.
When thou makest darkness and it is night,
all the beasts of the forest come forth. . . .
All of them look expectantly to thee
to give them their food at the proper time;
what thou givest them they gather up;
when thou openest thy hand, they eat their fill.
Then thou hidest thy face, and they are restless and
troubled;
when thou takest away their breath, they fail
and they return to the dust from which they came;
but when thou breathest into them, they recover;
thou givest new life to the earth.

— PSALM 104

I am that living and fiery Essence of the divine substance that glows in the beauty of the fields. I shine in the water, I burn in the sun, and the moon, and the stars. Mine is the mysterious force of the invisible wind. I permeate all things, that they may not die. I am Life.

— HILDEGARD OF BINGEN

Be praised, my Lord, for all your creatures.
In the first place for the blessed Brother Sun,
Who gives us the day and enlightens us through you.
Be praised, my Lord, for Sister Moon and the stars
Formed by you so bright, precious and beautiful.
Be praised, my Lord, for Brother Wind
And the airy skies, so cloudy and serene. . . .
Be praised, my Lord, for our sister, Mother Earth,
Who nourishes us and watches us
While bringing forth abundance of fruits with colored flowers
And herbs. . . .
Be praised, my Lord, for our sister, Bodily Death,
Who no living man can escape.
Praise and bless my Lord.
Render thanks.
Serve God with great humility.

— SAINT FRANCIS OF ASSISI

I am the self abiding
in the heart of all creatures;
I am their beginning,
their middle and their end.
Know that my brilliance,
flaming in the sun,
in the moon, and in fire,
illumines this whole universe.

— BHAGAVAD-GITA

The insect in the plant, the moth which spends its brief hours of existence hovering about the candle's flame—nay, the life which inhabits a drop of water, is as much an object of God's special providence as the mightiest monarch on his throne.

— HENRY BERGH, FOUNDER, ASPCA

O God, we thank thee
for all the creatures thou hast made,
so perfect in their kind—
great animals like the elephant and the rhinoceros,
humorous animals like the camel and the monkey,
friendly ones like the dog and the cat,
working ones like the horse and the ox,
timid ones like the squirrel and the rabbit,
majestic ones like the lion and the tiger,
for birds with their songs.
O God, give us such love for thy creation,
that love may cast out fear,
and all thy creatures—and thy creation—
see in men and women like us
their priest and their friend. . . .

—George Appleton

Love all God's creation, the whole universe, and each
grain of sand. Love every leaflet, every ray of God's light;
love the beasts, love the plants, love every creature. When
you love every creature, you will understand the mystery of
God in created things.

—Fyodor Dostoevski

We should understand well that all things are the work of the Great Spirit. We should know the Great Spirit is within all things: the trees, the grasses, the rivers, the mountains, and the four-legged and winged peoples; and even more important, we should understand that the Great Spirit is also above all these things and peoples. When we do understand all this deeply in our hearts, then we will fear, and love, and know the Great Spirit, and then we will be and act and live as the Spirit intends.

—BLACK ELK

We need another and wiser and perhaps more mystical concept of animals. We patronize them for their incompleteness, for their tragic fate of having taken form so far below ourselves. And therein we err, and greatly err. For the animal shall not be measured by man. In a world older and more complete than ours they move finished and complete, gifted with extensions of the senses we have lost or never attained, living by voices we shall never hear. They are not brethren; they are not underlings; they are other nations, caught with ourselves in the net of life and time, fellow prisoners of the splendour and the travail ahead.

—HENRY BESTON

All things bright and beautiful,
    All creatures great and small,
All things wise and wonderful,
    The Lord God made them all.

— CECIL FRANCES ALEXANDER

My Pet Hare

Yes—thou mayst eat thy bread, and lick the hand
That feeds thee; thou mayst frolic on the floor
At evening, and at night retire secure
To thy straw couch, and slumber unalarm'd;
For I have gain'd thy confidence, have pledged
All that is human in me, to protect
Thine unsuspecting gratitude and love.
If I survive thee, I will dig thy grave;
And, when I place thee in it, sighing say,
I knew at least one hare that had a friend.

—WILLIAM COWPER

No one has found a way to avoid death,
To pass around it;
Those old men who have met it,
Who have reached the place where death stands waiting,
Have not pointed out a way to circumvent it.
Death is difficult to face.

— OMAHA INDIANS

The Power of the Dog

There is sorrow enough in the natural way
From men and women to fill our day;
And when we are certain of sorrow in store,
Why do we always arrange for more?
Brothers and Sisters, I bid you beware
Of giving your heart to a dog to tear.

When the body that lived at your single will,
With its whimper of welcome, is stilled (how still!),
When the spirit that answered your every mood
Is gone—whether it goes—for good,
You will discover how much you care,
And will give your heart to a dog to tear.

— RUDYARD KIPLING

Pass to thy Rendezvous of Light,
Pangless except for us—
Who slowly ford the Mystery
Which thou hast leaped across!

— EMILY DICKINSON

———•———

Do not stand at my grave and weep.
I am not there, I do not sleep.
I am a thousand winds that blow.
I am the diamond glint on snow.
I am the sunlight on ripened grain.
I am the gentle autumn rain. When you wake in the
                                    morning hush,
    I am the swift, uplifting rush
    Of quiet birds in circling flight.
    I am the soft starlight at night.
Do not stand at my grave and weep.
I am not there. I do not sleep.

— ANONYMOUS

Nothing is ever really lost, or can be lost,
No birth, identity, form—no object of the world,
Nor life, nor force, nor any visible thing;
Appearance must not foil, nor shifted sphere confuse
 thy brain.
Ample are time and space—ample the fields of Nature.

—WALT WHITMAN

Deep peace of the running wave
 to you.
Deep peace of the flowing air
 to you.
Deep peace of the quiet earth
 to you.
Deep peace of the shining stars
 to you.
Deep peace of the infinite peace
 to you.

—ADAPTED FROM GAELIC RUNES

Of Jeoffry, His Cat

For I will consider my Cat Jeoffry.

For he is the servant of the Living God, duly and daily
serving him.

For at the first glance of the glory of God in the East he
worships in his way.

For this is done by wreathing his body seven times round
with elegant quickness.

For then he leaps up to catch the musk, which is the
blessing of God upon his prayer.

For he rolls upon prank to work it in.

For having done duty and received blessing he begins to
consider himself.

For this he performs in ten degrees.

For first he looks upon his fore-paws to see if they are clean.

For secondly he kicks up behind to clear away there.

For thirdly he works it upon stretch with the fore-paws
extended.

For fourthly he sharpens his paws by wood.

For fifthly he washes himself.

For sixthly he rolls upon wash.

For seventhly, he fleas himself, that he may not be inter-
rupted upon the beat.

For eighthly he rubs himself against a post.

For ninthly he looks up for his instructions.

For tenthly he goes in quest of food.

For having consider'd God and himself he will consider his
          neighbor. . . .

For God has blessed him in the variety of his movements.

For, tho' he cannot fly, he is an excellent clamberer.

For his motions upon the face of the earth are more than
          any other quadrupede.

For he can tread to all the measures upon the musick.

For he can swim for life.

For he can creep.

— CHRISTOPHER SMART

In the house of long life
I will wander.
In the house of happiness
I will wander.
With beauty before me
I will wander.
With beauty behind me
I will wander.
With beauty above me
I will wander.
With beauty below me
I will wander. In old age traveling
On the trail of beauty
I will wander.
It shall be finished in beauty.

— NIGHT CHANT OF THE NAVAJO

What is life? It is the flash of a firefly in the
night. It is the breath of a buffalo in the winter time.
It is the little shadow which runs across the grass
and loses itself in the sunset.

—CROWFOOT, CHIEF OF THE BLACKFEET NATION

There is not a beast on earth, nor fowl that
flieth on two wings, but they are a people like
unto you, and to God they shall return.

— THE KORAN

Know, first, that heaven, and earth's compacted frame,
And flowing waters, and the starry frame,
And both the radiant lights, one common soul
Inspires and feeds—and animates the whole.
This active mind, infused through all space,
Unites and mingles with the mighty mass:
Hence, men and beasts the breath of life obtain,
And birds of air, and monsters of the main.
Th'ethereal vigour is in all the same,
And every soul is filled with equal flame.

— VIRGIL'S *AENEID*,
TRANSLATED BY JOHN DRYDEN

ONE FAMILY'S RITUAL OF LEAVETAKING

Remembering Lady
Loving companion, wise teacher—
and forever the playful retriever!

—Errol G. Sowers

When the vet told us our beloved twelve-year-old golden retriever had less than two months to live, we were not exactly surprised. The tumor in the middle of her back was quickly metastasizing and growing bigger every day. This condition, combined with severe arthritis in Lady's rear legs, did not portend good news. Still, her now-imminent death pained our hearts.

The next six weeks were filled with both joy and sadness. Lady, too, somehow knew that every day was to be savored. So despite her increasing discomfort, she pushed us to play her favorite game—retrieving thrown rocks. And each time we played, the vitality of youth seemed to return, if only for a few moments.

Days before the tumor was ready to erupt through the skin, the vet arrived at our home, medical bag in hand. We had decided to make Lady's last few hours a time of honoring her life and being fully present during her transition. Little did we know that this gift would contribute most to our own healing.

While we didn't plan a formal ceremony, my wife, Meredith, son Mark, and two close friends, Jeremy and Helena, gathered with me on a sunny hillside less than fifty feet from the open grave we had dug earlier. Together we created a memorial service that embraced these four elements:

1. *Honoring the Life Lived:* As we sat on the ground, I held Lady so her head rested gently in my lap. With everyone taking turns stroking her, we reminisced about the times we shared with her. With tears flowing freely down my cheeks, I recalled Lady's frequent nuzzling of my hand and the little four-footed dance she always did with a few barks thrown in whenever she wanted to play her "retrieval game." Meredith recalled the proud way she took a territorial stand accompanied by constant barking every time a strange dog so much as dared venture onto our property. Even the stories about her occasional digging in our flower gardens brought back fond memories.

2. *Giving Reassurance:* With no doubt in our minds, Lady knew her time in this physical world was drawing to a close. She gave me one long last look with those soft brown eyes as if to say, "It's okay. I'm ready. I'm not afraid. And thanks for being with me before I go back home." In seeking to reassure her, we found ourselves being the ones reassured. Being present when euthanasia is chosen by an animal's caretaker is absolutely an act of kindness as well as balm for lessening one's own grief and suffering.

3. *Releasing to the Oneness of Life:* As Mark and I carried her quiet limp body and placed it lovingly into the earth, we felt a gentle lifting of our spirits as if God were more

present than usual. The energy in the air was palpable, and we knew deep inside that all would be well. In those few moments of committing a loved one's body back to Mother Earth, we realized how precious life really is and at the same time knew that we are all inextricably connected to each other and to the Creator.

4. *Remembering with Love:* Our animal friends are great teachers. They participate easily in the flow of life and surely accept death with greater courage than most of us humans. As we reflected on this experience of life, death, and—we believe, rebirth—we felt richly blessed and filled with a deep sense of community. Lady's spirit was tangibly present. It was as if we would feel her laughing again, freed from a worn-out body and forever the playful retriever.

BIBLIOGRAPHY

Auden, W.H. "Talking to Dogs," *Harper's,* 242 (March 1971).

Bly, Robert. *News of the Universe: poems of twofold consciousness.* San Francisco: Sierra Club Books, 1980.

Butler, Carolyn, Suzanne Hetts, and Laurel Lagoni. *Friends for Life: Loving and Losing Your Animal Companion.* Boulder, Colorado: Sounds True Audio, 1996.

Cantwell, Mary. "The Soul Knows No Species, Nor Does Love." *New York Times* (March 22, 1990).

Clinebell, Howard. *Basic Types of Pastoral Care and Counseling.* Nashville: Abingdon Press, 1984.

Frey, William. *Crying: The Mystery of Tears.* Minneapolis: Winston Press, 1985.

Galsworthy, John. *Memories.* New York: Charles Scribner's Sons, 1914.

Gould, Stephen Jay. "Our Allotted Lifetimes." *Natural History* (No. 7, 1977).

Goodman, Jacki. *The Fireside Book of Dog Stories.* New York: Simon and Schuster, 1943.

Grollman, Earl. *Talking About Death: A Dialogue Between Parent and Child.* Boston: Beacon Press, 1976.

Joseph, Richard. *A Letter To The Man Who Killed My Dog.* New York: Frederick Fell, 1956.

Kahn, Robbie Pfeufer. "Though It's Your Heart's Passion: Healing From The Death of a Family Dog." A paper presented to the Refereed Roundtable, Sociology of Emotions, American Sociological Association, New York, 1996.

Katcher, Aaron, and Alan Beck. "Health and Caring for Living Things." *Anthrozoos* 1 (No. 3, 1987).

Katcher, Aaron (ed.). *New Perspectives on Our Lives with Companion Animals.* Philadelphia: University of Pennsylvania Press, 1983.

Keillor, Garrison. "The Poetry Judge." *The Atlantic Monthly* 277 (February 1996).

Keillor, Garrison. *We Are Still Married.* New York: Penguin Books, 1990.

Kenworthy, Jack. *Dog Training Guide.* London: Pet Library Ltd., 1969.

Kipling, Rudyard. *Collected Dog Stories.* Garden City, NY: Doubleday, Doran & Co., 1934.

Kübler-Ross, Elisabeth. *Death is of Vital Importance.* Barrytown, NY: Station Hill Press, 1995.

Kutner, L. "For Children, the Death of a Pet Isn't Practice for Something More Serious; It's the Real Thing." *New York Times* (August 2, 1990).

Lee, Laura. "Coping with Pet Loss." *Dogs Today* 6 (September 1996).

Levinson, Boris. "Acute Grief in Animals." *Archives of the Foundation of Thanatology* 9 (No. 2, 1981).

Lewis, Richard (ed.). *Miracles: Poems by children of the English-speaking world.* New York: Simon and Schuster, 1966.

McKeown, Donal, D.V.M., and Earl Strimple, D.V.M. *Your Pet's Health from A to Z.* New York: Robert B. Luce Co., Inc., 1973.

Mason, Jim. *An Unnatural Order.* New York: Continuum, 1997.

Matthews, Peter (ed.). *The Guinness Book of Records.* New York: Bantam Books, 1995.

Meyer, Richard E., and David M. Gradwolh. "Best Damm Dog We Ever Had: Some Folkloristic and Anthropological Observations on San Francisco's Presidio Pet Cemetery." *Markers XII: Journal of the Association for Gravestone Studies* (Vol. 12, 1995).

Nieburg, Herbert, and Arlene Fischer. *Pet Loss: A Thoughtful Guide for Adults and Children.* New York: Harper & Row, 1982.

Nuland, Sherwin. *How We Die: Reflections on Life's Final Chapter.* New York: Alfred A. Knopf, 1994.

Patterson, Francine, and Eugene Linden. *The Education of Koko.* New York: Holt, Rinehart & Winston, 1981.

Porter, Valerie. *Faithful Companions: The Alliance of Man and Dog.* London: Methuen, 1987.

Searl, Edmund. *In Memoriam: A Guide to Modern Funeral and Memorial Services.* Boston: Skinner House, 1993.

Serpell, James. *In the Company of Animals: A Study of Human-Animal Relationships.* New York: B. Blackwell, 1986.

Temerlin, Maurice K. *Lucy: Growing Up Human.* Palo Alto, CA: Science and Behavior Books, 1975.

May we recommend:

The Souls of Animals

BY GARY KOWALSKI

"Gary Kowalski helps us unlock the mysteries of animal spirituality. For as we have learned from the companion animals that share our lives and our homes, when we look into their eyes we see the reflection of our own humanity."

 —KIM STALLWOOD, Editor
  The Animals' Agenda

"Gary Kowalski's voice is one that empowers us to say in public what we have thought in private—that animals love their companions, know grief and joy, and play and create. They are truly our brothers and sisters in fur, feather and fin."

 —TOM REGAN, author of
  The Case for Animal Rights

"This is an important book because it is so revealing of the animal soul that touches ours when we are open and receptive. In the process, our own souls are enriched."

 —DR. MICHAEL W. FOX, Vice President
  The Humane Society of the United States